FLIGHT

FLIERS AND FLYING MACHINES

Series Editor:
David Salariya was born in Dundee, Scotland, where he studied illustration and printmaking, concentrating on book design in his postgraduate year. He later completed a further postgraduate course in art education at Sussex University in England. He has illustrated a wide range of books on botanical, historical and mythical subjects. He has designed and created many new series of children's books for publishers in the United Kingdom and overseas. In 1989, he established his own publishing company, The Salariya Book Company Ltd. He lives in Brighton, England, with his wife, illustrator Shirley Willis.
Author:
David Jefferis learned to fly before he could drive a car. Inspired by his enthusiasm for all things to do with aviation, space, science and futurology, he has written over twenty children's books on aeronautics. He also designs books and magazines and spends his spare time hang gliding and canoeing.

Consultant:
Andrew Nahum is a curator in the Science Museum, London. He has written extensively on transport subjects.

Series Editor	David Salariya
Book Editor	Vicki Power
Design Assistant	Carol Attwood
Consultant	Andrew Nahum
Artists	Mark Bergin Nick Hewetson John James Tony Townsend Hans Wiborg-Jenssen Gerald Wood

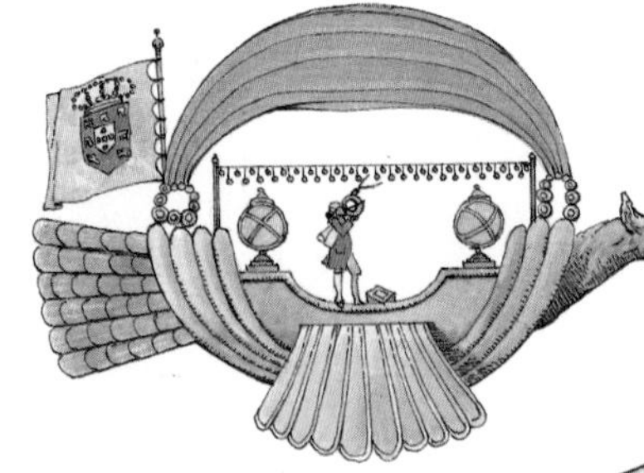

First published in 1991
by Franklin Watts

Franklin Watts, Inc.
387 Park Avenue South
New York, NY 10016

Typeset by Central Southern Typesetters (Hove) Ltd

Printed in Belgium

Artists

Mark Bergin, p 4–5, p 12–13, p 20–21, p 22–23, p 24–25, p 26–27, p 28–29; **Nick Hewetson**, p 18–19; **John James**, p 32–33; **Tony Townsend**, p 36–37, p 38–39, p 42–43; **Hans Wiborg-Jenssen**, p 34–35, p 40–41; **Gerald Wood**, p 6–7, p 8–9, p 10–11, p 14–15, p 16–17, p 30–31.

Library of Congress Cataloging-in-Publication Data
Jefferis, David.
Flight/David Jefferis.
p. cm. – (Timelines)
Includes Index.
Summary: Traces the evolution of the airplane from man's first flying machine to today's supersonic jets.
ISBN 0-531-15233-2- –ISBN 0-531-11093-1 (lib. bdg.)
1. Airplanes – Juvenile literature [1. Airplanes.] I. Title.
II. Series: Timelines
TL547.J44 1991
629.13'09--dc20 91-7801
CIP AC

TIMELINES

FLIGHT

FLIERS AND FLYING MACHINES

Written by
DAVID JEFFERIS

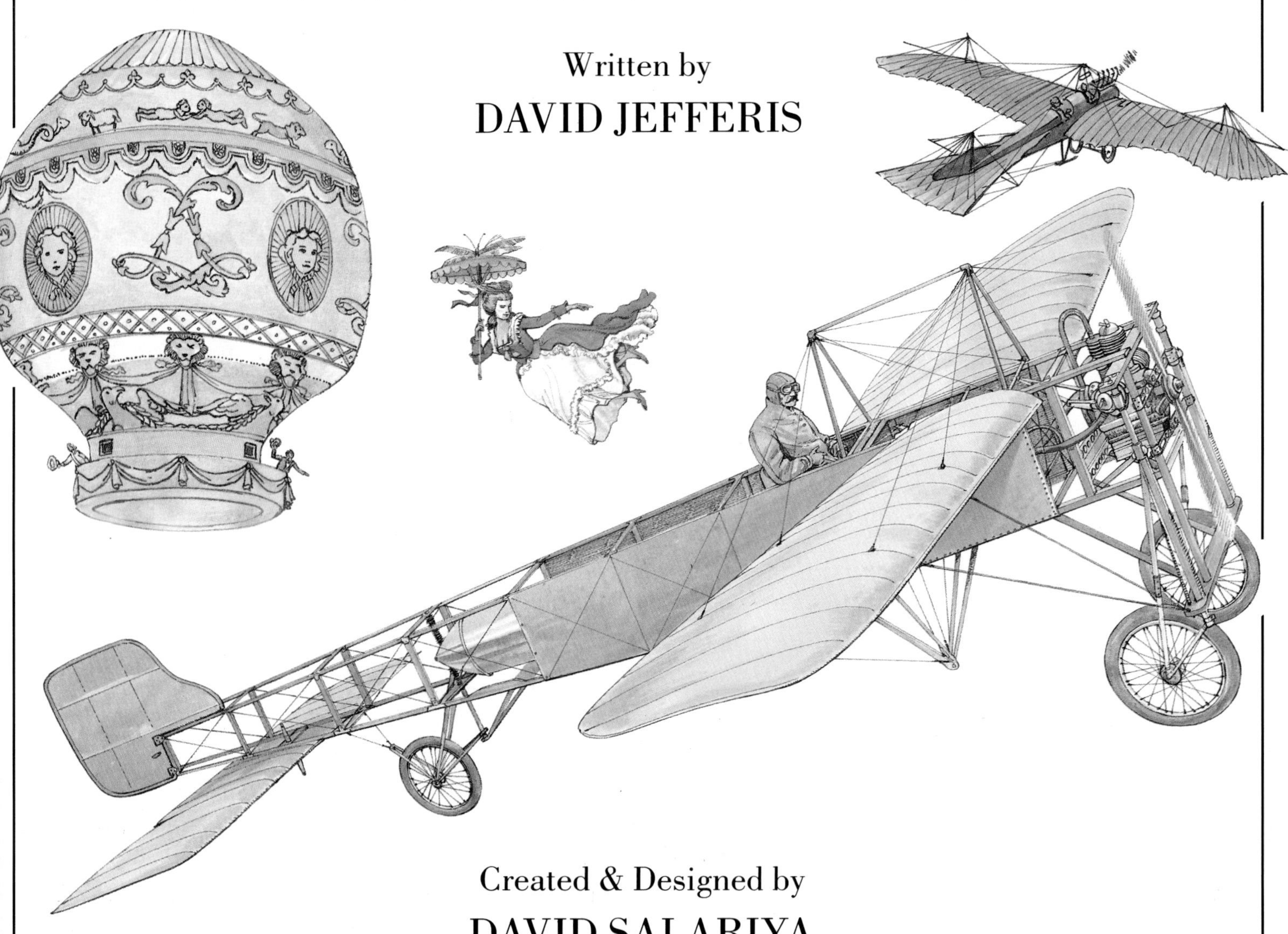

Created & Designed by
DAVID SALARIYA

FRANKLIN WATTS
New York • London • Toronto • Sydney

Contents

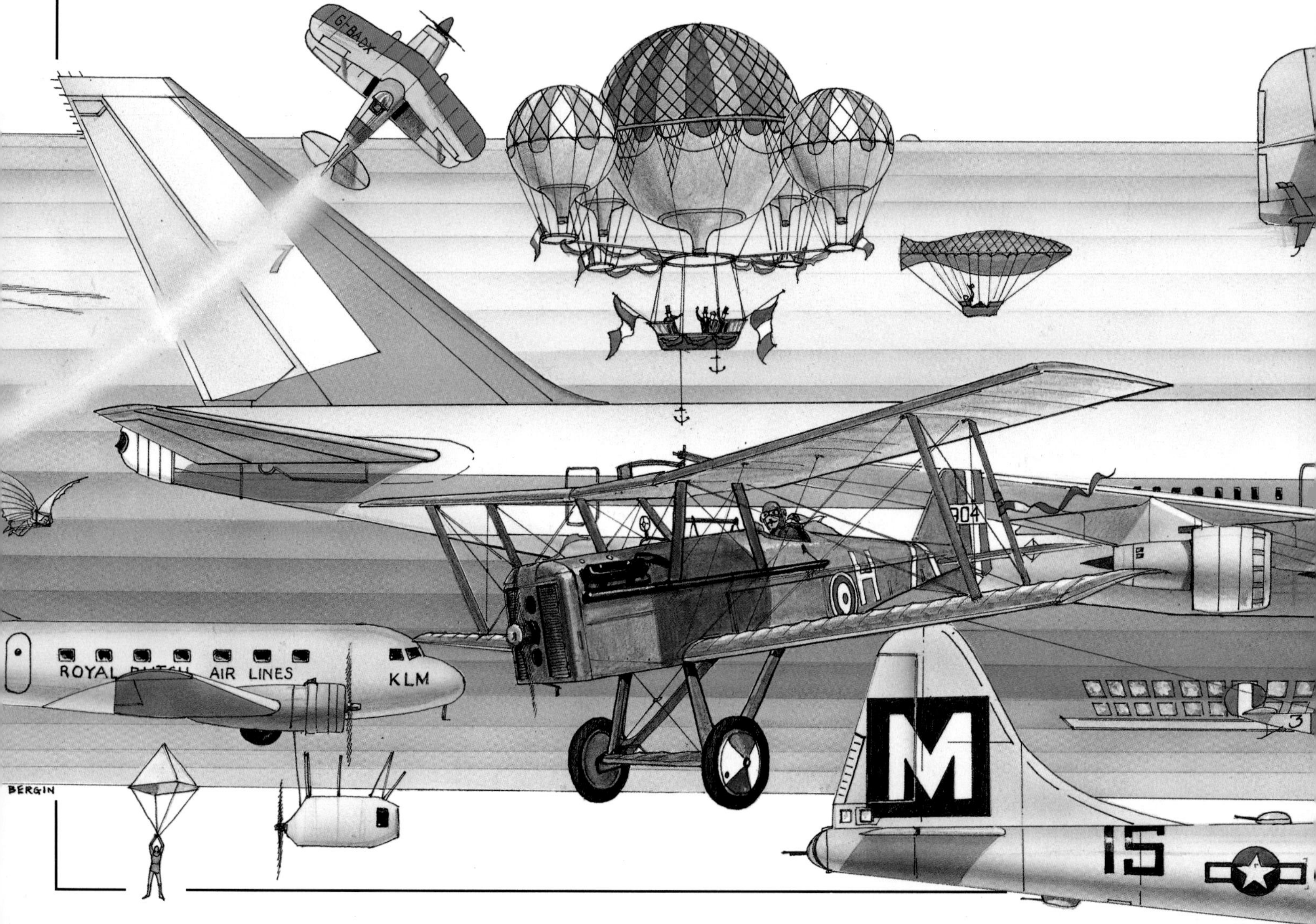

DREAMS OF FLIGHT

THE IDEA OF FLYING GOES BACK thousands of years. There are dozens of flight legends, including the myth of *Icarus* and *Daedalus*, two Greeks who made wax and feather wings to escape from the island of Crete. The story goes that Icarus flew too high, the wax in his wings melted in the sun, and he fell to his death. Daedalus flew lower and landed in Sicily. This was a legend, but copying the birds seemed a good idea to many would-be fliers.

▽ BIRD FLIGHT was the main inspiration for the early dreamers, but all their attempts ended in failure.

△ DAEDALUS AND HIS SON ICARUS during their mythical flight. Hang gliders are the nearest thing modern aviation has to wings of wax.

△ A BIRD'S TAKE-OFF STROKE forces air to flow over the wings. Surging power strokes then accelerate the bird forward through the air. Its tail acts as a rudder and balance weight.

Imitating bird flight was a complete failure for several good reasons, the main one being their very high power-to-weight ratio. That is, birds have a lot of muscle power for their size, lifting very little weight. Compared with the birds, our arm and shoulder muscles are puny, and our bodies and bones heavy and solid. Flapping-wing flight is simply not possible for a human.

A bird's easy flight was not therefore a good model for human fliers. It was not until the 19th century that the idea of fixed wings became the basis for successful manned flight.

Bird flight is a complex mixture of wing movements, matched by an equally complex set of moment-by-moment body and tail adjustments to provide the fine balance control required.

▽ THE 11TH CENTURY English monk Eilmer of Malmesbury managed to glide from a tower.

△ LEONARDO'S flying machine would have been far too heavy to have been a success.

▽ 17TH CENTURY ITALIAN Francesco de Lana drew this machine, with vacuum spheres for lift.

Throughout the Middle Ages, inventors dreamed up ideas for flying machines. In about 1488, Leonardo da Vinci sketched out a flapping-wing machine, or ornithopter. If it had been built (*above*) it could have weighed 600 pounds (272 kg) or more, over four times the weight of the pilot. Ideas like this, and others such as Laurenço de Gusmão's mysterious machine (below) were doomed to failure.

▷ A PORTUGUESE PRIEST, Laurenço de Gusmão, designed the *Passarola* or "Great Bird" in 1709. De Gusmão never revealed the principles involved, but some historians believe lifting power was supplied by powerful magnets.

◁ IN 1678, THE FRENCHMAN BESNIER WAS supposed to have made a gliding flight using a pair of large wooden wings.

▽ A TRIO OF SPANISH oarsmen was the power source suggested for this 18th century flying fish of Joseph Patinho.

BALLOONS

THE FIRST MANNED FLIGHTS WERE IN HOT AIR BALLOONS. During the 18th century Jacques and Joseph Montgolfier experimented with smoke-filled paper bags. They thought that rising smoke was a lifting force, and in 1783 succeeded in getting a 35-foot (10.7-meter) wide bag to leave the ground. In September of that year, they sent a sheep, a duck and a cockerel aloft to become the first animal aviators. On November 21, the Marquis d'Arlandes and Jean Pilâtre de Rozier climbed aboard a Montgolfier balloon. Their manned flight, the first ever, lasted 25 minutes and they rose 500 feet (152 meters) into the air.

△ IN DECEMBER 1783, the first hydrogen-filled balloon made an ascent under the command of French physicist Jacques César Charles. The balloon was made of rubber-coated silk and floated a distance of about 25 miles (40 km).

△ COLORFUL balloons, of many shapes and sizes floated through the skies of 18th and 19th century Europe.

△ ONE OF THE SIGHTS of 1798 was that of balloonist Monsieur Margat sitting on a white stag called Coco, while floating over Paris.

△ IN 1830, a Mrs. Graham was saved by her billowing skirt as she fell from a balloon.

◁ LEONARDO'S sketch for a parachute (*left*) and a design from Hungary (*above*).

The idea of a parachute probably dates from sketches drawn by Leonardo da Vinci in about 1500. The first actual parachute descent was made by a daring Frenchman, André Garnerin, in 1797. He dropped from a balloon floating some 7,000 feet (2135 m) above the streets of Paris.

△ FRENCHMAN André Garnerin made a safe parachute drop from a balloon in 1797.

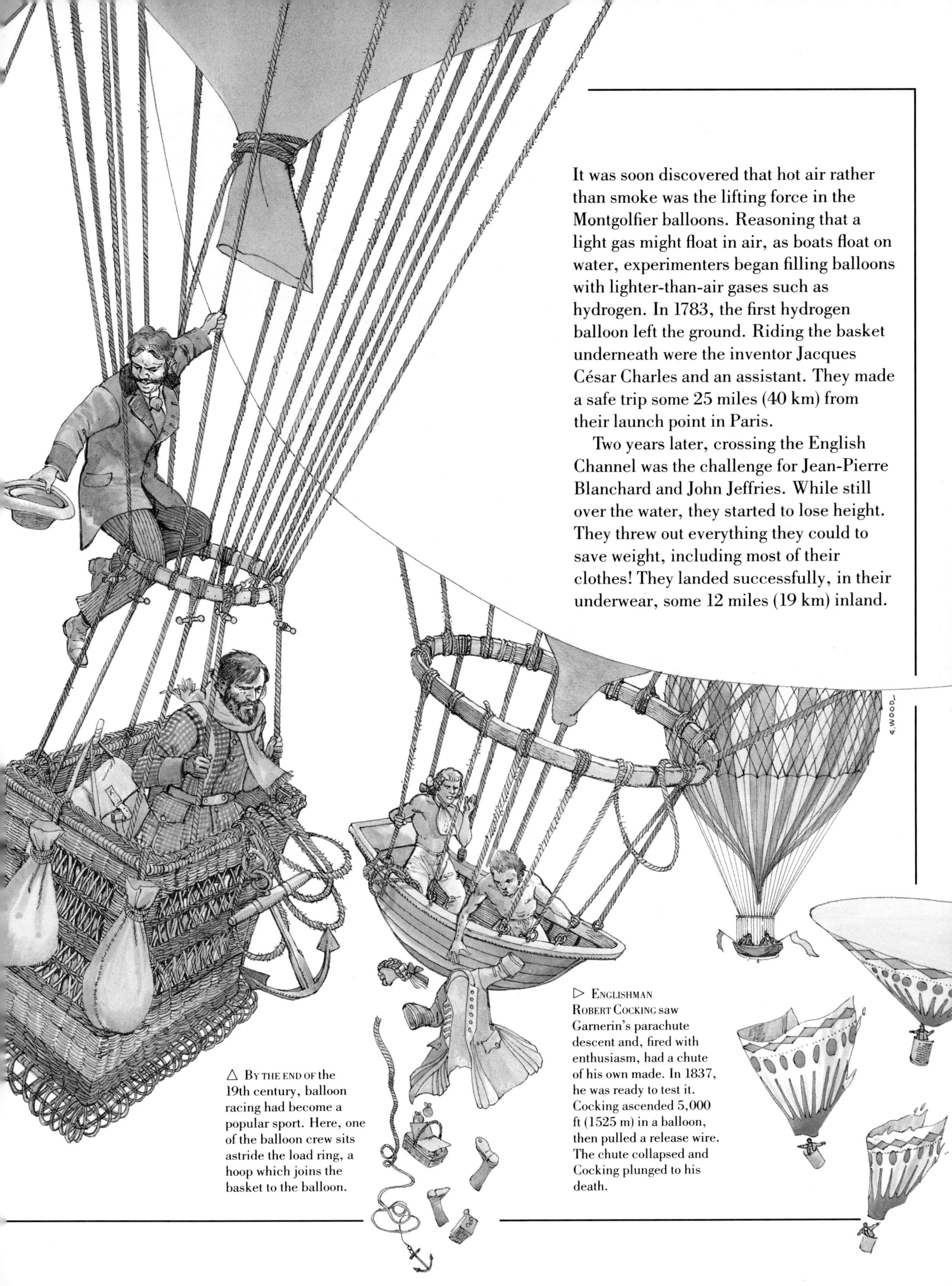

It was soon discovered that hot air rather than smoke was the lifting force in the Montgolfier balloons. Reasoning that a light gas might float in air, as boats float on water, experimenters began filling balloons with lighter-than-air gases such as hydrogen. In 1783, the first hydrogen balloon left the ground. Riding the basket underneath were the inventor Jacques César Charles and an assistant. They made a safe trip some 25 miles (40 km) from their launch point in Paris.

Two years later, crossing the English Channel was the challenge for Jean-Pierre Blanchard and John Jeffries. While still over the water, they started to lose height. They threw out everything they could to save weight, including most of their clothes! They landed successfully, in their underwear, some 12 miles (19 km) inland.

△ BY THE END OF the 19th century, balloon racing had become a popular sport. Here, one of the balloon crew sits astride the load ring, a hoop which joins the basket to the balloon.

▷ ENGLISHMAN ROBERT COCKING saw Garnerin's parachute descent and, fired with enthusiasm, had a chute of his own made. In 1837, he was ready to test it. Cocking ascended 5,000 ft (1525 m) in a balloon, then pulled a release wire. The chute collapsed and Cocking plunged to his death.

Gliding

THE 1800s SAW THE DAWN OF FLIGHT AS WE KNOW IT. Though balloons were successful enough, they had their limitations, not least that of being blown in whatever direction the wind took them. The man who is the father of present day flight was the English engineer Sir George Cayley. All his ideas stemmed from the small model glider he made in 1804. This had a fixed wing and a movable tailplane, features found in aircraft ever since. Once the idea of flapping wings was abandoned, it was a short step to making gliding flights.

Cayley's success included his triplane glider of 1849, which flew with a small boy aboard. Four years later, when Cayley was 80, he sent one of his coachmen on a gliding flight on the grounds of his home in Yorkshire. It is said that the coachman, unamused, promptly resigned after landing safely. Successful as Cayley's gliders were, they lacked one thing – a suitable engine.

△ KITES were first invented by the Chinese.

△ IN 1889 AMERICAN INVENTOR R.J. Spalding came up with this design for an "ornithopter," a flapping-wing flying machine. The design never made it to a finished stage, and Spalding seems to have had little confidence in his device. His plans called for a balloon to be attached to help keep it in the air.

△ A 1799 SKETCH of Cayley's fixed-wing glider.

▽ SIR GEORGE CAYLEY'S GLIDERS pioneered many of the designs seen in today's planes.

◁ CAYLEY'S triple-wing glider of 1849 had a wheeled undercarriage and tailplane for steering. Flights were launched downhill and also by towing with a rope, when the glider took off like a kite. The glider made two successful flights, carrying a 10-year old boy as a nervous "pilot".

▷ FOUR YEARS after his "boy glider," Cayley made a monoplane, with one of his coachmen as an unwilling pilot.

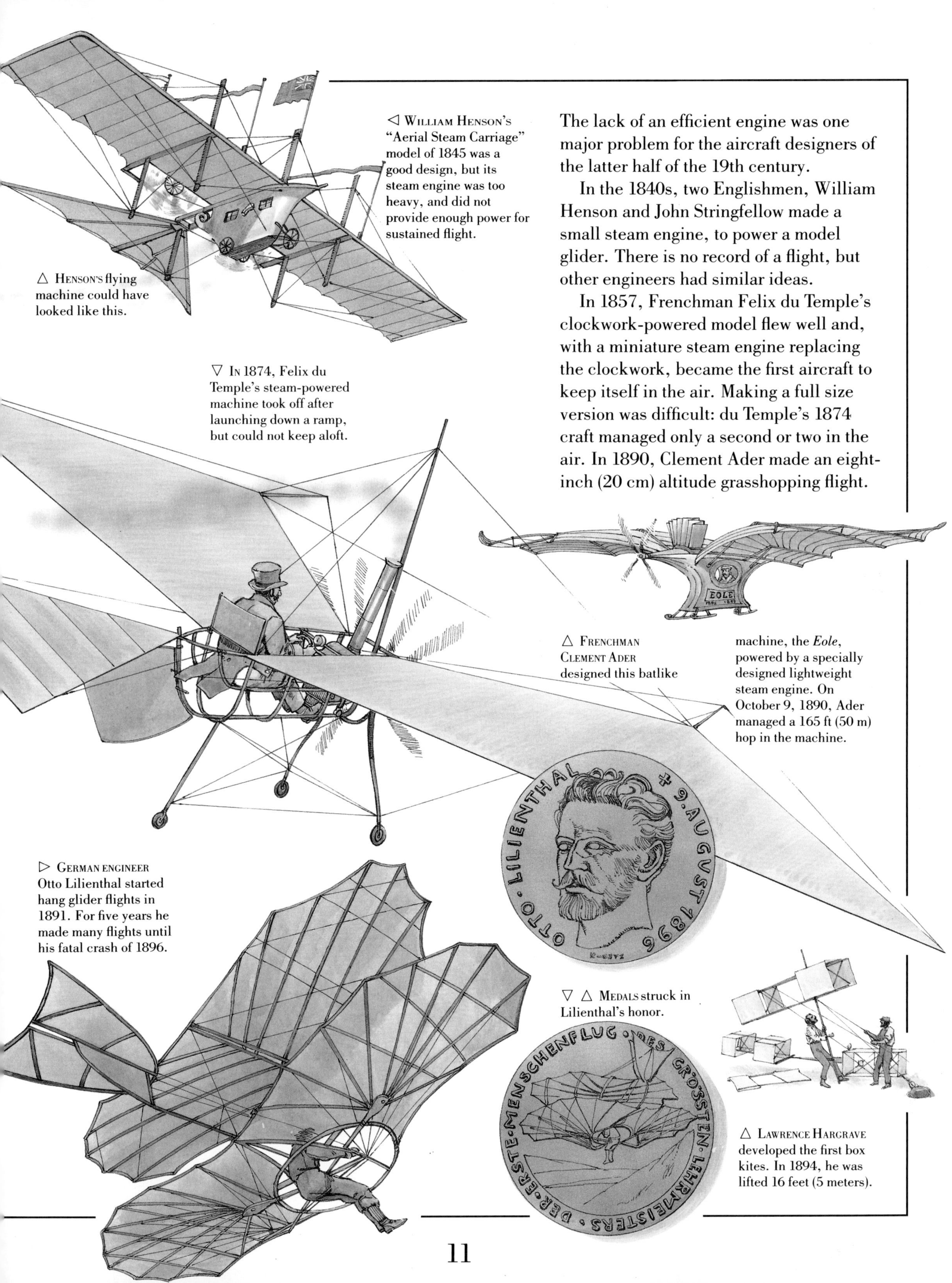

△ Henson's flying machine could have looked like this.

◁ William Henson's "Aerial Steam Carriage" model of 1845 was a good design, but its steam engine was too heavy, and did not provide enough power for sustained flight.

The lack of an efficient engine was one major problem for the aircraft designers of the latter half of the 19th century.

In the 1840s, two Englishmen, William Henson and John Stringfellow made a small steam engine, to power a model glider. There is no record of a flight, but other engineers had similar ideas.

In 1857, Frenchman Felix du Temple's clockwork-powered model flew well and, with a miniature steam engine replacing the clockwork, became the first aircraft to keep itself in the air. Making a full size version was difficult: du Temple's 1874 craft managed only a second or two in the air. In 1890, Clement Ader made an eight-inch (20 cm) altitude grasshopping flight.

▽ In 1874, Felix du Temple's steam-powered machine took off after launching down a ramp, but could not keep aloft.

△ Frenchman Clement Ader designed this batlike machine, the *Eole*, powered by a specially designed lightweight steam engine. On October 9, 1890, Ader managed a 165 ft (50 m) hop in the machine.

▷ German engineer Otto Lilienthal started hang glider flights in 1891. For five years he made many flights until his fatal crash of 1896.

▽ △ Medals struck in Lilienthal's honor.

△ Lawrence Hargrave developed the first box kites. In 1894, he was lifted 16 feet (5 meters).

The Wright Brothers

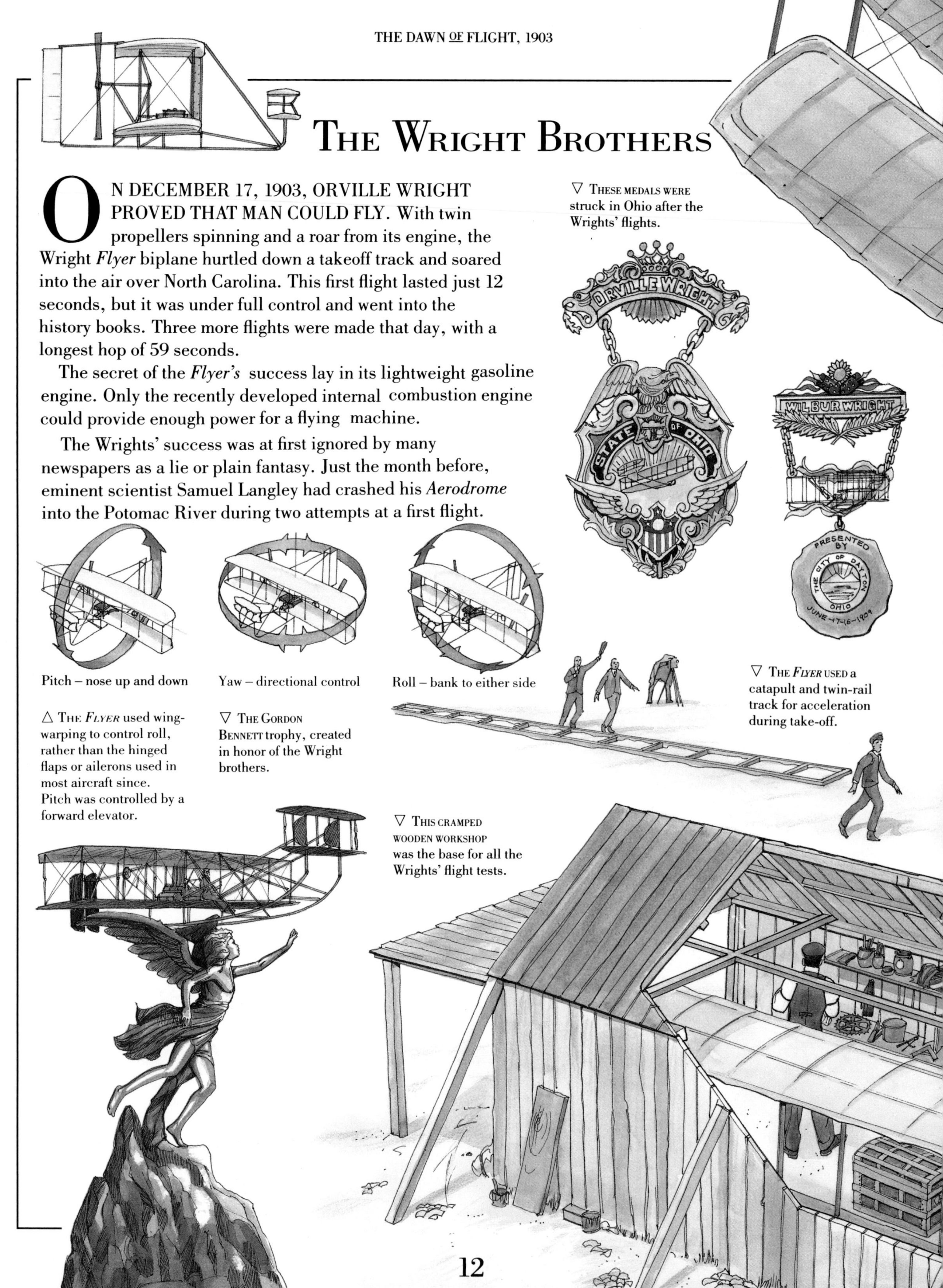

ON DECEMBER 17, 1903, ORVILLE WRIGHT PROVED THAT MAN COULD FLY. With twin propellers spinning and a roar from its engine, the Wright *Flyer* biplane hurtled down a takeoff track and soared into the air over North Carolina. This first flight lasted just 12 seconds, but it was under full control and went into the history books. Three more flights were made that day, with a longest hop of 59 seconds.

The secret of the *Flyer's* success lay in its lightweight gasoline engine. Only the recently developed internal combustion engine could provide enough power for a flying machine.

The Wrights' success was at first ignored by many newspapers as a lie or plain fantasy. Just the month before, eminent scientist Samuel Langley had crashed his *Aerodrome* into the Potomac River during two attempts at a first flight.

▽ These medals were struck in Ohio after the Wrights' flights.

Pitch – nose up and down

Yaw – directional control

Roll – bank to either side

△ The *Flyer* used wing-warping to control roll, rather than the hinged flaps or ailerons used in most aircraft since. Pitch was controlled by a forward elevator.

▽ The Gordon Bennett trophy, created in honor of the Wright brothers.

▽ The *Flyer* used a catapult and twin-rail track for acceleration during take-off.

▽ This cramped wooden workshop was the base for all the Wrights' flight tests.

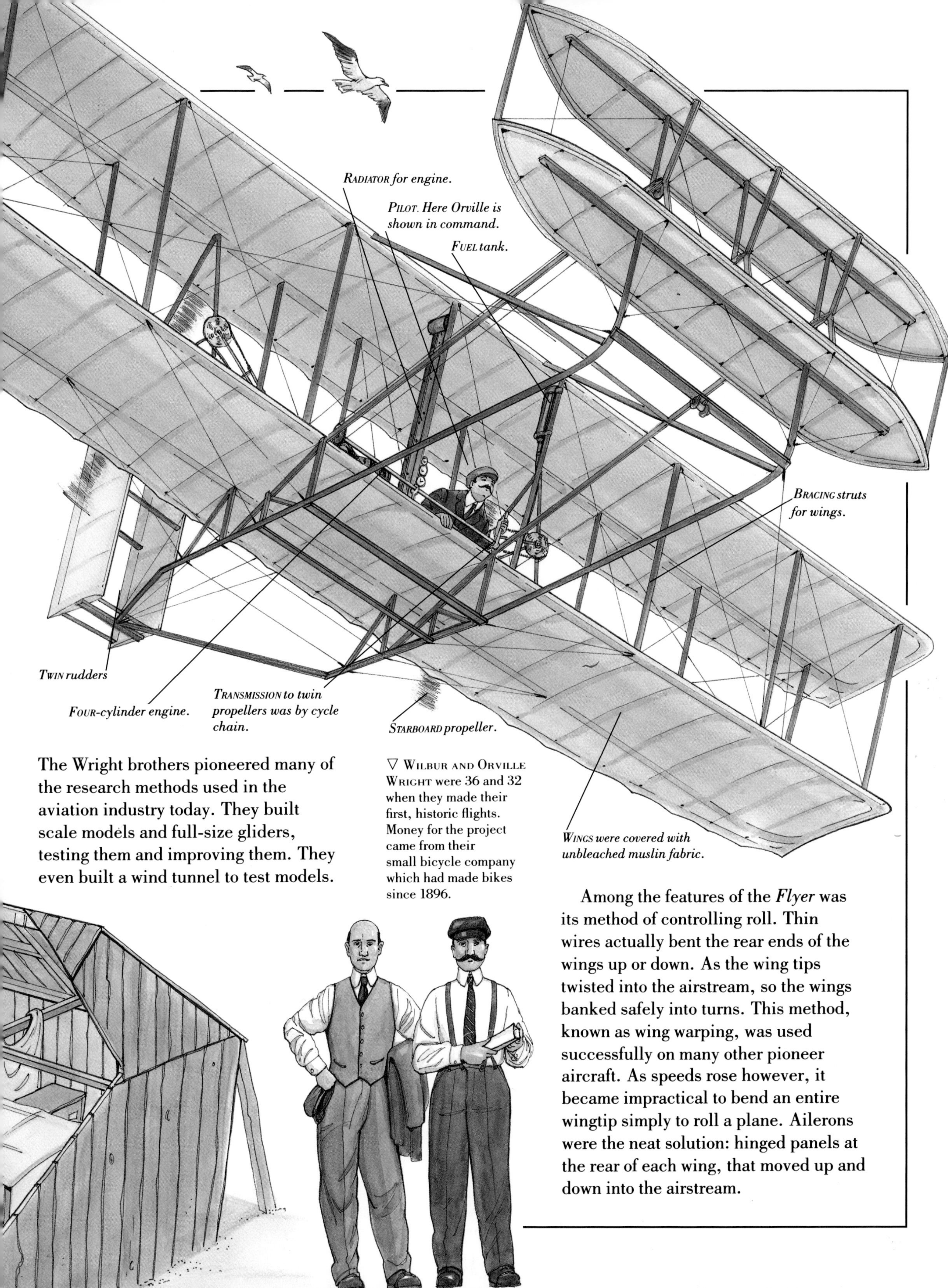

The Wright brothers pioneered many of the research methods used in the aviation industry today. They built scale models and full-size gliders, testing them and improving them. They even built a wind tunnel to test models.

▽ WILBUR AND ORVILLE WRIGHT were 36 and 32 when they made their first, historic flights. Money for the project came from their small bicycle company which had made bikes since 1896.

Among the features of the *Flyer* was its method of controlling roll. Thin wires actually bent the rear ends of the wings up or down. As the wing tips twisted into the airstream, so the wings banked safely into turns. This method, known as wing warping, was used successfully on many other pioneer aircraft. As speeds rose however, it became impractical to bend an entire wingtip simply to roll a plane. Ailerons were the neat solution: hinged panels at the rear of each wing, that moved up and down into the airstream.

First Aviators

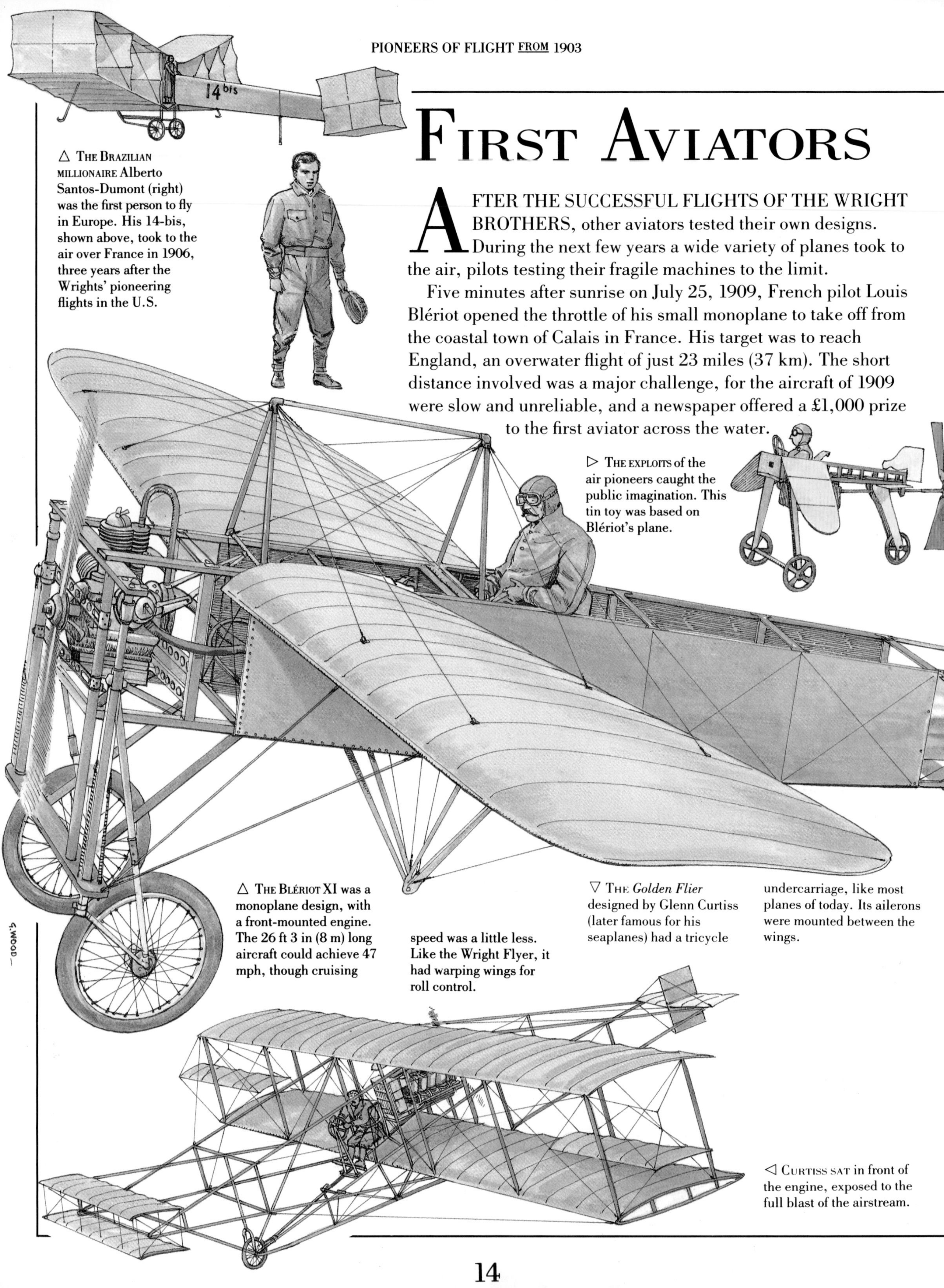

△ The Brazilian millionaire Alberto Santos-Dumont (right) was the first person to fly in Europe. His 14-bis, shown above, took to the air over France in 1906, three years after the Wrights' pioneering flights in the U.S.

After the successful flights of the Wright Brothers, other aviators tested their own designs. During the next few years a wide variety of planes took to the air, pilots testing their fragile machines to the limit.

Five minutes after sunrise on July 25, 1909, French pilot Louis Blériot opened the throttle of his small monoplane to take off from the coastal town of Calais in France. His target was to reach England, an overwater flight of just 23 miles (37 km). The short distance involved was a major challenge, for the aircraft of 1909 were slow and unreliable, and a newspaper offered a £1,000 prize to the first aviator across the water.

▷ The exploits of the air pioneers caught the public imagination. This tin toy was based on Blériot's plane.

△ The Blériot XI was a monoplane design, with a front-mounted engine. The 26 ft 3 in (8 m) long aircraft could achieve 47 mph, though cruising speed was a little less. Like the Wright Flyer, it had warping wings for roll control.

▽ The *Golden Flier* designed by Glenn Curtiss (later famous for his seaplanes) had a tricycle undercarriage, like most planes of today. Its ailerons were mounted between the wings.

◁ Curtiss sat in front of the engine, exposed to the full blast of the airstream.

Blériot's flight across the English Channel was a complete success, though not without its moments of tension. Soon after leaving France, Blériot lost sight of land and flew way off course. He spotted the English coast in time to head for Dover and landed on the cliff tops above the town.

The Blériot XI which made the journey was advanced for its time, with a single-wing monoplane construction.

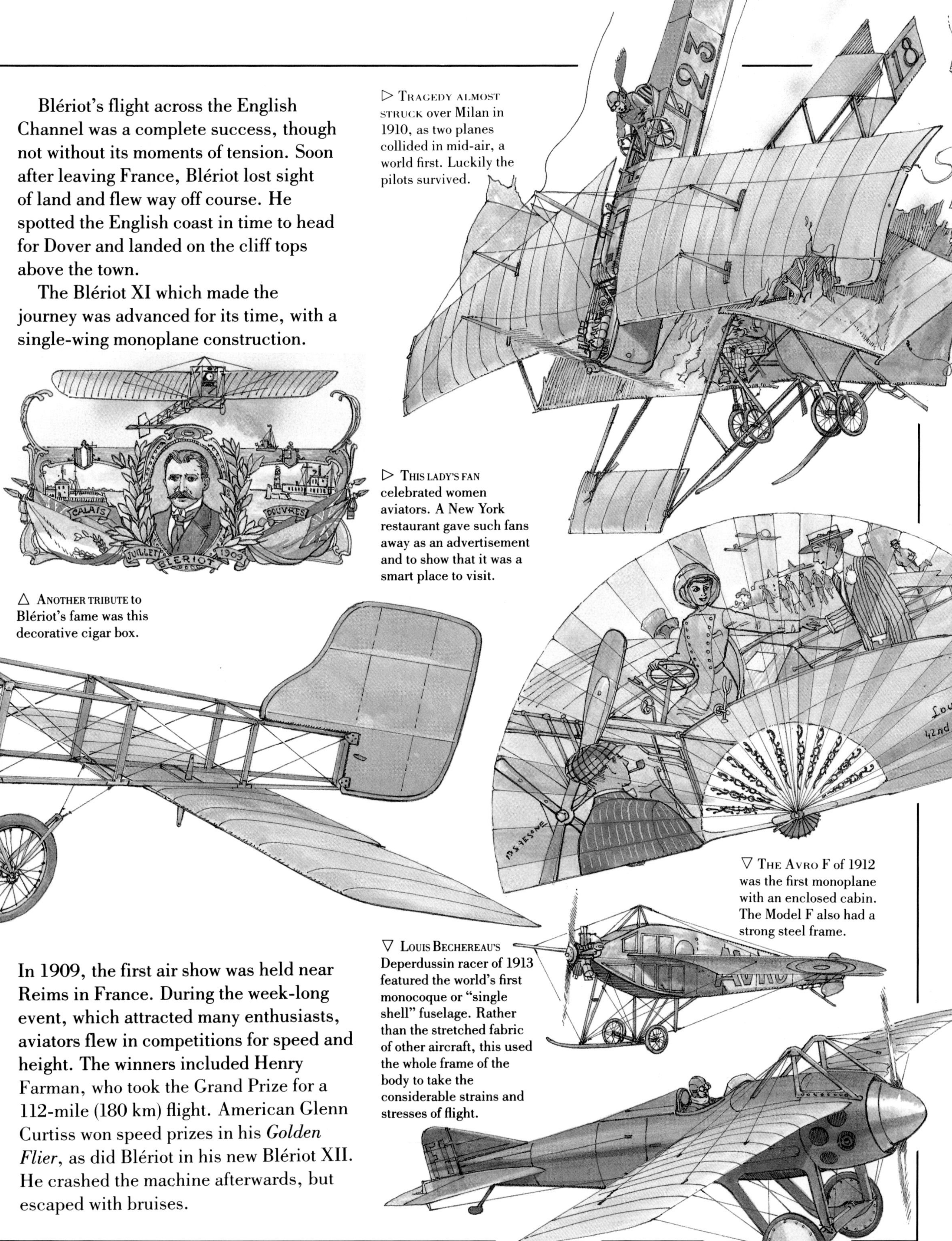

▷ TRAGEDY ALMOST STRUCK over Milan in 1910, as two planes collided in mid-air, a world first. Luckily the pilots survived.

▷ THIS LADY'S FAN celebrated women aviators. A New York restaurant gave such fans away as an advertisement and to show that it was a smart place to visit.

△ ANOTHER TRIBUTE to Blériot's fame was this decorative cigar box.

▽ THE AVRO F of 1912 was the first monoplane with an enclosed cabin. The Model F also had a strong steel frame.

▽ LOUIS BECHEREAU'S Deperdussin racer of 1913 featured the world's first monocoque or "single shell" fuselage. Rather than the stretched fabric of other aircraft, this used the whole frame of the body to take the considerable strains and stresses of flight.

In 1909, the first air show was held near Reims in France. During the week-long event, which attracted many enthusiasts, aviators flew in competitions for speed and height. The winners included Henry Farman, who took the Grand Prize for a 112-mile (180 km) flight. American Glenn Curtiss won speed prizes in his *Golden Flier*, as did Blériot in his new Blériot XII. He crashed the machine afterwards, but escaped with bruises.

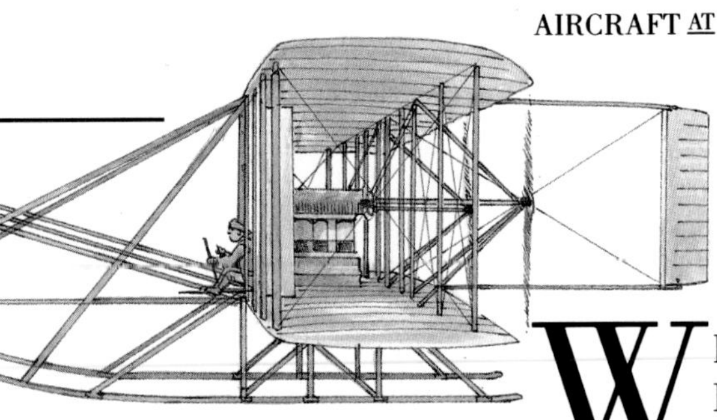

World War I

WHEN WORLD WAR I OPENED IN 1914, most aircraft were little more than fragile toys. By the war's end four long years later, military aircraft had evolved into fast and efficient fighting machines.

The Wright Military Flyer of 1909 had paved the way for army aviation. An upgraded version of the original Flyer, it had an extra seat for an observer or gunner and carried out successful weapon firing trials. The British B.S.1 test aircraft of 1913 featured many of the details that appeared on fighters in the war.

The first bombs were dropped from a German Taube, a bird-like aircraft that was very stable in flight. The pilot could take his hands off the controls for long enough to throw a small bomb over the side at enemy troops.

△ The Wright Military Flyer of 1909 was a two-seater, with room for an observer or gunner in addition to the pilot.

△ Samuel Cody became Britain's first aviator in 1908 when he flew (and crashed) his British Army Aeroplane No 1.

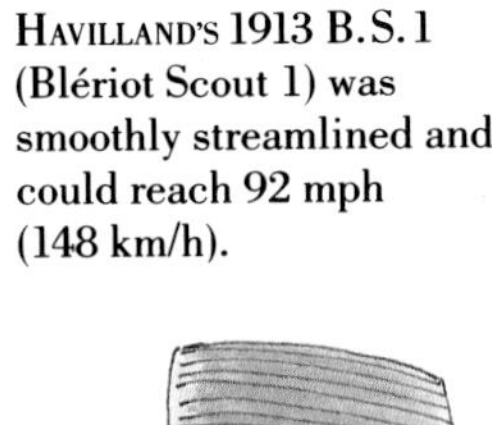

▽ Geoffrey de Havilland's 1913 B.S.1 (Blériot Scout 1) was smoothly streamlined and could reach 92 mph (148 km/h).

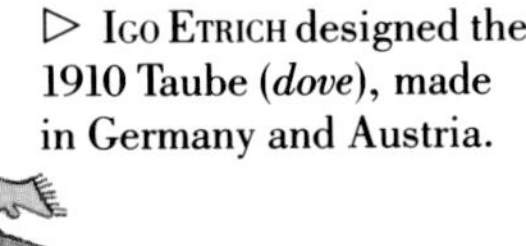

▷ Igo Etrich designed the 1910 Taube (*dove*), made in Germany and Austria.

▷ Flying gear had advanced since the boiler suit worn by Louis Blériot. The main needs were for windproofing and warmth. Sheepskin and leather were the best materials to defeat frostbite at high altitudes. Goggles were essential eye protection, while boots and gloves warmed hands and feet.

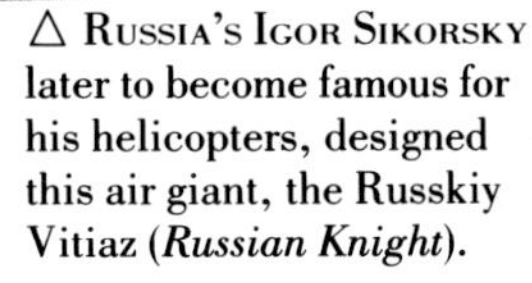

△ Russia's Igor Sikorsky later to become famous for his helicopters, designed this air giant, the Russkiy Vitiaz (*Russian Knight*). The four-engined machine first flew in May 1913 to become the first successful big aircraft. At full throttle, it could just reach 60 mph (97 km/h).

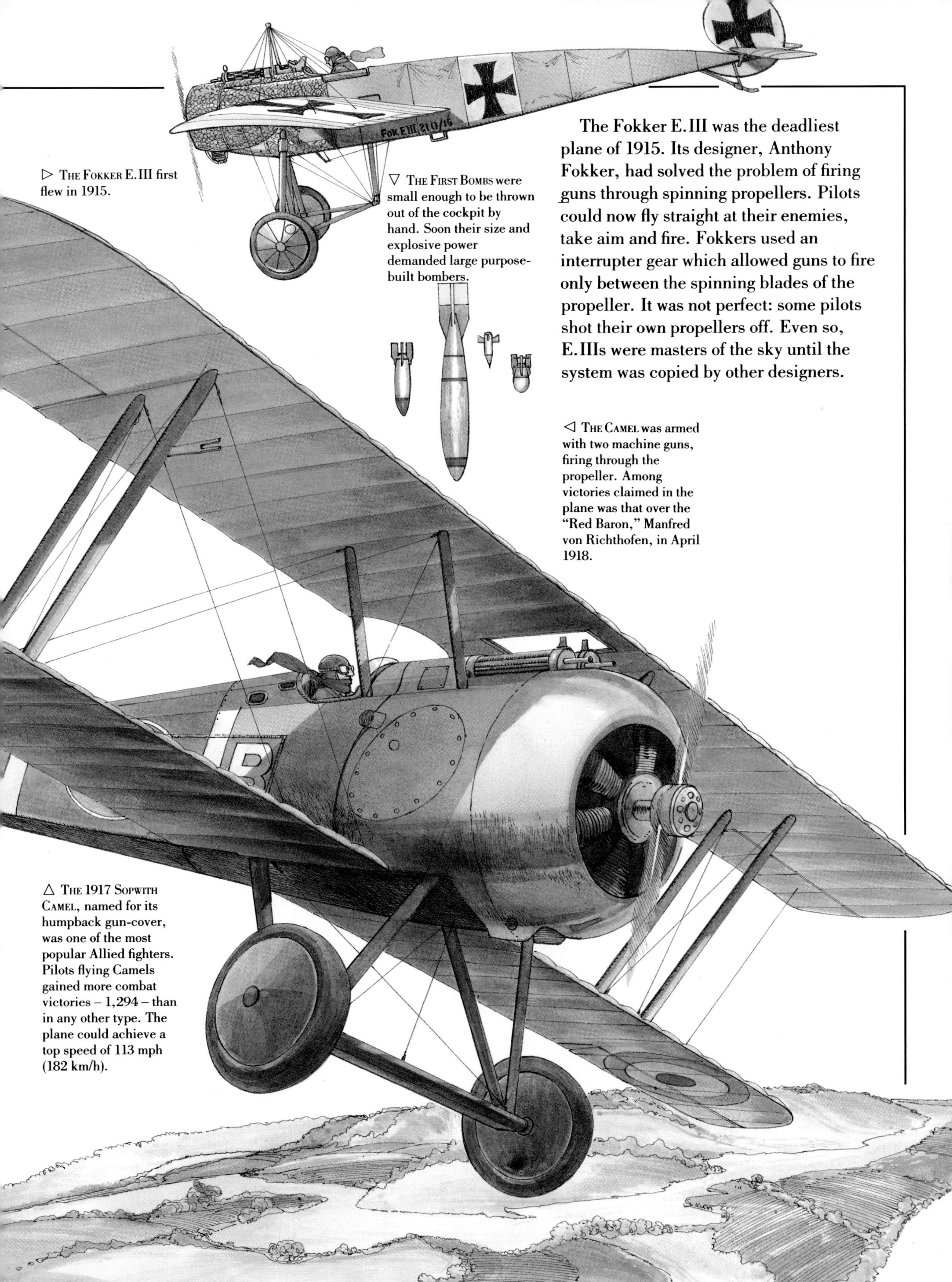

The Fokker E.III was the deadliest plane of 1915. Its designer, Anthony Fokker, had solved the problem of firing guns through spinning propellers. Pilots could now fly straight at their enemies, take aim and fire. Fokkers used an interrupter gear which allowed guns to fire only between the spinning blades of the propeller. It was not perfect: some pilots shot their own propellers off. Even so, E.IIIs were masters of the sky until the system was copied by other designers.

▷ The Fokker E.III first flew in 1915.

▽ The First Bombs were small enough to be thrown out of the cockpit by hand. Soon their size and explosive power demanded large purpose-built bombers.

◁ The Camel was armed with two machine guns, firing through the propeller. Among victories claimed in the plane was that over the "Red Baron," Manfred von Richthofen, in April 1918.

△ The 1917 Sopwith Camel, named for its humpback gun-cover, was one of the most popular Allied fighters. Pilots flying Camels gained more combat victories – 1,294 – than in any other type. The plane could achieve a top speed of 113 mph (182 km/h).

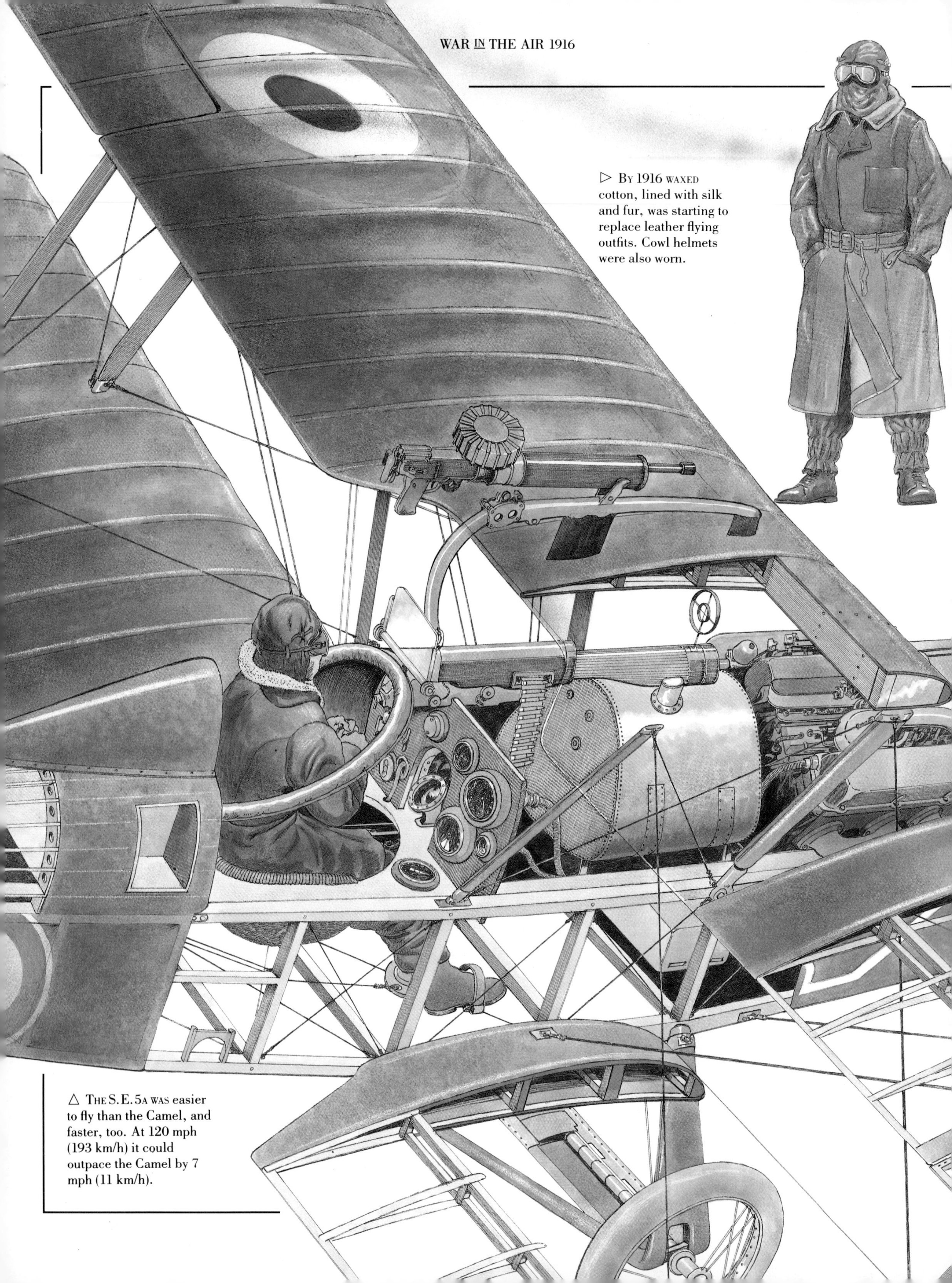

▷ BY 1916 WAXED cotton, lined with silk and fur, was starting to replace leather flying outfits. Cowl helmets were also worn.

△ THE S.E.5A WAS easier to fly than the Camel, and faster, too. At 120 mph (193 km/h) it could outpace the Camel by 7 mph (11 km/h).

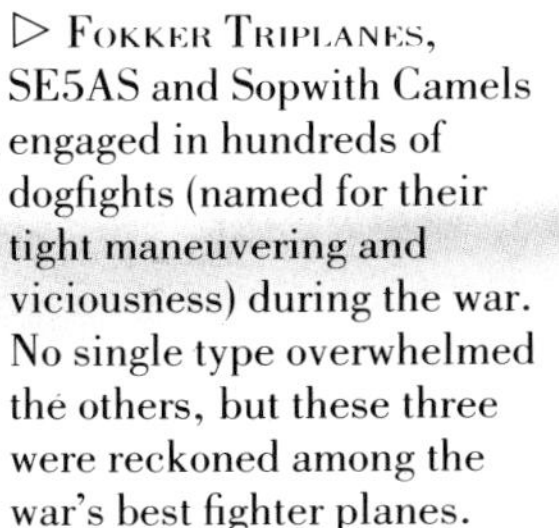

▷ FOKKER TRIPLANES, SE5AS and Sopwith Camels engaged in hundreds of dogfights (named for their tight maneuvering and viciousness) during the war. No single type overwhelmed the others, but these three were reckoned among the war's best fighter planes.

AIR BATTLES

AS THE WAR ROLLED ON, AIR COMBAT BECAME A GRIM BUSINESS. In the early days, few pilots were armed with more than a service revolver. This soon stopped when both sides tried to stop enemy observation and bombing missions. In 1917 the flying time of new combat pilots was reckoned in bare hours before they were shot down. Few pilots had parachutes: military commanders considered that their use discouraged bravery.

▷ THE FOKKER DR.I TRIPLANE was made famous by the exploits of von Richthofen, the Red Baron. The aircraft was fast and nimble in close combat.

Two of the best fighter planes of the war were the German Fokker Drl Triplane (*above*) and the British S.E.5a (*left*). The Triplane gained fame in the skilled hands of the ace flier Manfred von Richthofen, the "Red Baron." Between autumn 1916 and spring 1918, the Baron downed 80 enemy aircraft, the highest tally of any pilot in the war. Von Richthofen painted his own plane bright red, and encouraged the pilots who flew under his command to paint their own machines in similarly gaudy colors. The much feared squadron, Jasta 11, was nicknamed the "flying circus" by allied fliers. But even the best pilot of the war was not invulnerable, and von Richthofen was shot down and killed on April 21, 1918.

The S.E.5a was a workmanlike aircraft, easy to fly and a very stable gun platform. It had a new type of interrupter mechanism, that worked by oil pressure, simpler and more reliable than the old mechanical linkage. Over 5,200 S.E.5s and S.E.5as were built and the plane was flown by leading British ace Edward "Mick" Mannock, who notched up 73 victories.

◁ THE S.E.5A COULD BE armed with a Lewis gun mounted on the top wing that could fire forward or upward. With skill, a pilot could swoop below an enemy aircraft and rake its belly with deadly fire. The guns of most planes jammed frequently, and many pilots were shot down.

AIRSHIPS

THE VAST PASSENGER-CARRYING AIRSHIPS of the German Zeppelin company were successors to those used for reconnaissance and bombing in World War I. In the 1920s, the technology that had gone into warfare went to produce luxury airships of the sky.

The *Graf Zeppelin* shown here was the most successful of these airships, and in 1929 flew the amazing distance of 7,000 miles (11,270 km) from its home base in Friedrichshafen to Tokyo, Japan. The airship continued in passenger service across the Atlantic Ocean until the beginning of World War II.

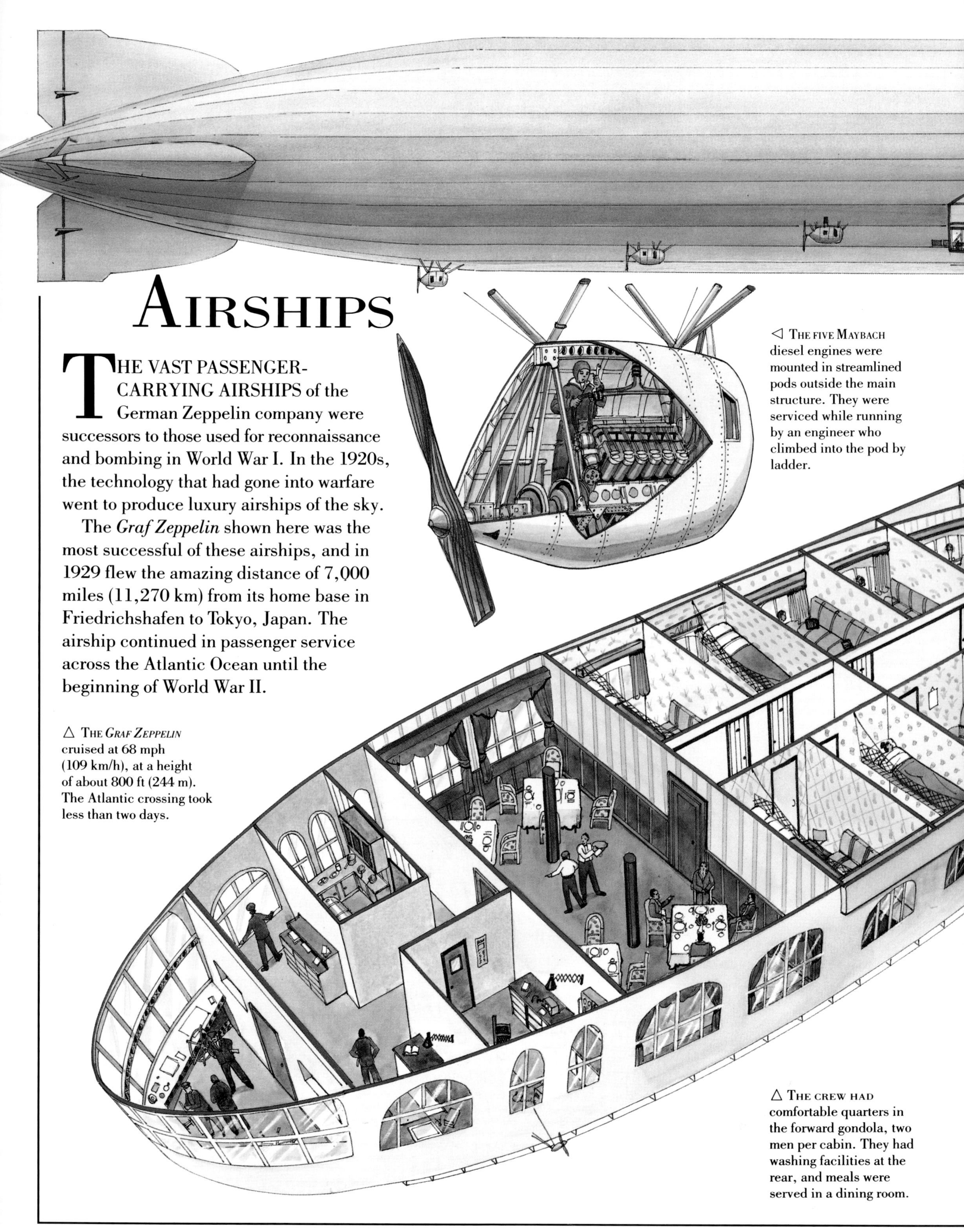

△ THE *GRAF ZEPPELIN* cruised at 68 mph (109 km/h), at a height of about 800 ft (244 m). The Atlantic crossing took less than two days.

◁ THE FIVE MAYBACH diesel engines were mounted in streamlined pods outside the main structure. They were serviced while running by an engineer who climbed into the pod by ladder.

△ THE CREW HAD comfortable quarters in the forward gondola, two men per cabin. They had washing facilities at the rear, and meals were served in a dining room.

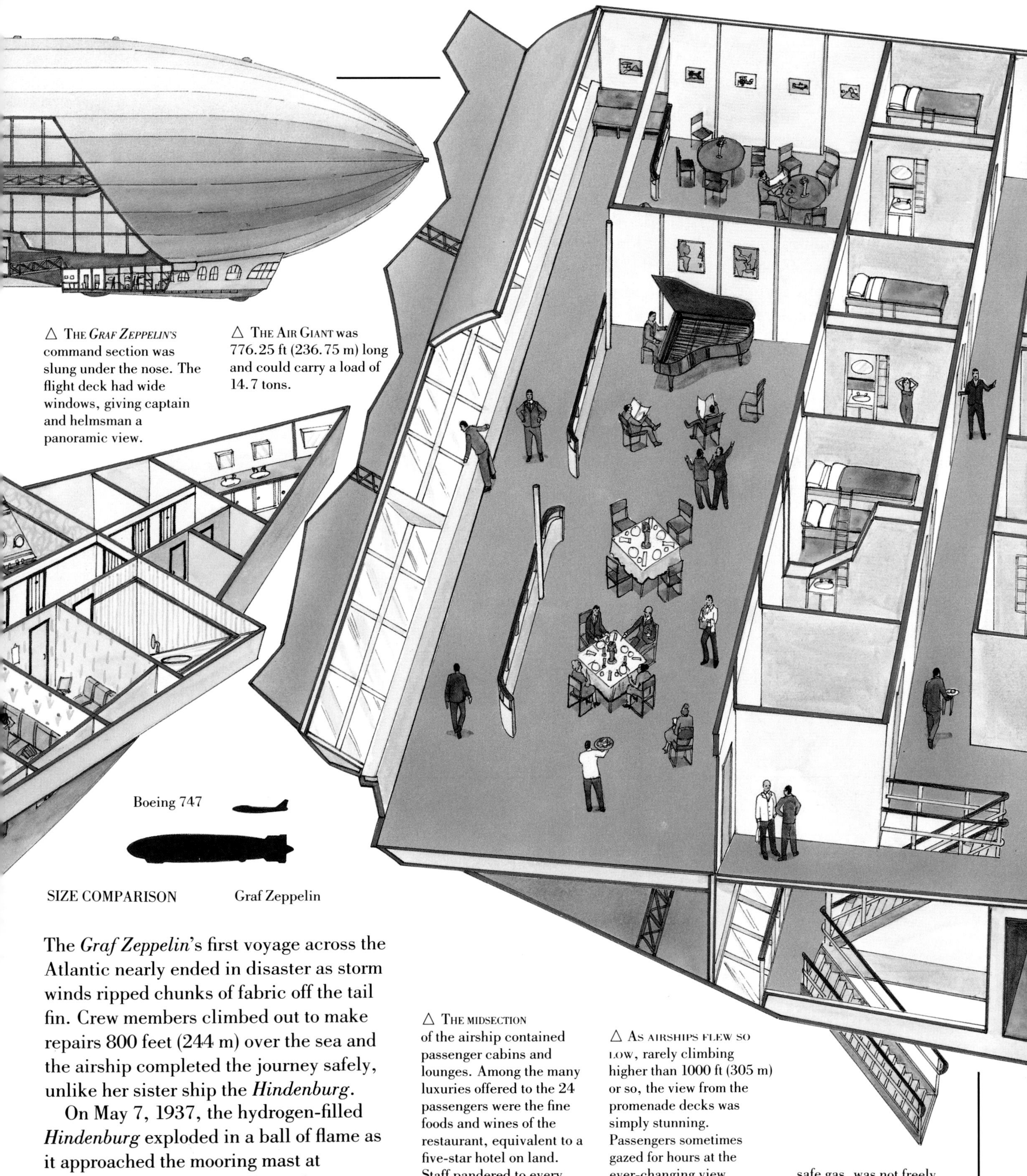

△ The *Graf Zeppelin's* command section was slung under the nose. The flight deck had wide windows, giving captain and helmsman a panoramic view.

△ The Air Giant was 776.25 ft (236.75 m) long and could carry a load of 14.7 tons.

The *Graf Zeppelin*'s first voyage across the Atlantic nearly ended in disaster as storm winds ripped chunks of fabric off the tail fin. Crew members climbed out to make repairs 800 feet (244 m) over the sea and the airship completed the journey safely, unlike her sister ship the *Hindenburg*.

On May 7, 1937, the hydrogen-filled *Hindenburg* exploded in a ball of flame as it approached the mooring mast at Lakehurst, New Jersey. Thirty-five crew and passengers were killed, a number considered horrific enough in the 1930s to finish off the age of the airship.

△ The midsection of the airship contained passenger cabins and lounges. Among the many luxuries offered to the 24 passengers were the fine foods and wines of the restaurant, equivalent to a five-star hotel on land. Staff pandered to every need, and there was even a grand piano, made of aluminium, to provide music while eating and for dancing later.

△ As airships flew so low, rarely climbing higher than 1000 ft (305 m) or so, the view from the promenade decks was simply stunning. Passengers sometimes gazed for hours at the ever-changing view below. Like its sister ship, the *Hindenburg*, *Graf Zeppelin* used flammable hydrogen gas to provide lift. Helium, a safe gas, was not freely available at the time. Cigarette and pipe smoking was banned on board, except in a metal-lined fireproof room.

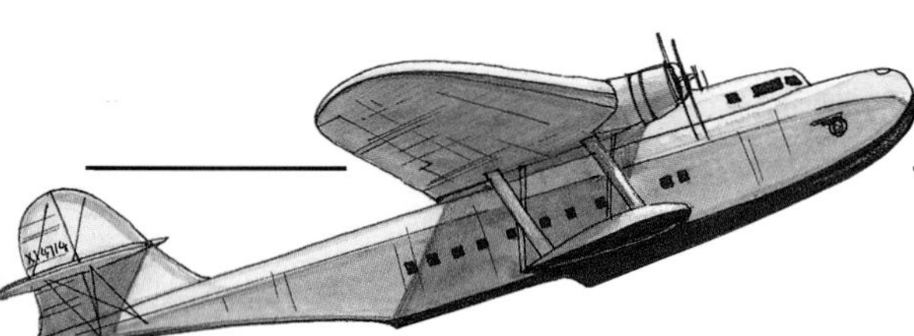

Flying Boats

FLYING BOATS WERE QUEENS OF THE AVIATION WORLD THROUGHOUT THE 1930s. They were big and comfortable, so were ideal for long distance travel. Harbors were also airports in the thirties. Flying boats could taxi to shelter and drop anchor. The passengers and crew members were then just a few minutes' boat ride away from a hotel.

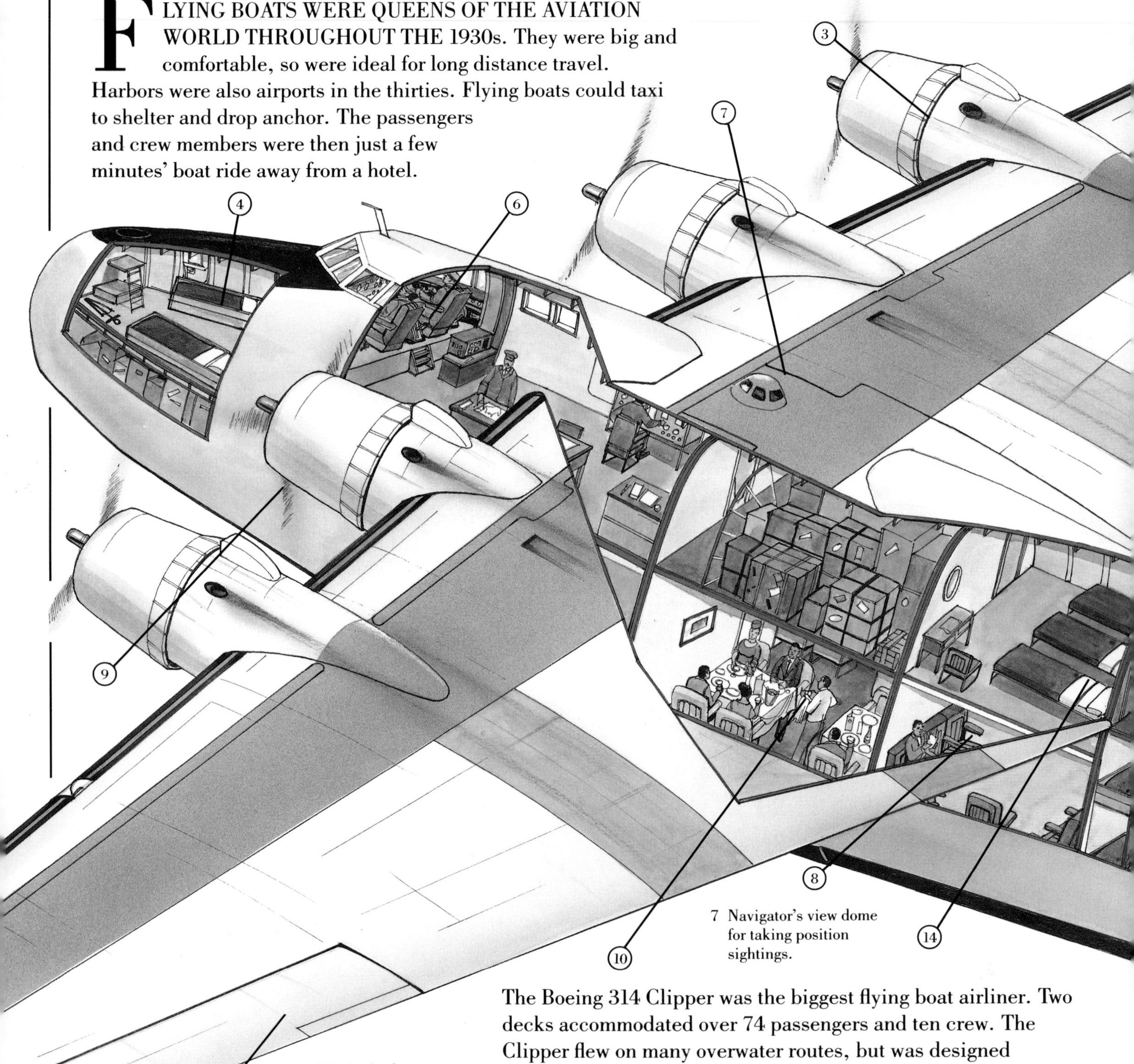

The Boeing 314 Clipper was the biggest flying boat airliner. Two decks accommodated over 74 passengers and ten crew. The Clipper flew on many overwater routes, but was designed especially for flights across the Atlantic. During such flights, navigators looked out of a clear dome, noting star positions to check the plane's course, just as if they were on board a ship. The transatlantic flight was quicker than going by liner but could still take 20 hours or more, cruising at about 180 mph.

Key
1 Port (left) aileron.
2 All-metal construction.
3 Wright Cyclone engine, one of four.
4 Crew's day cabin and anchor.
5 Baggage compartments.
6 Cockpit area.
7 Navigator's view dome for taking position sightings.

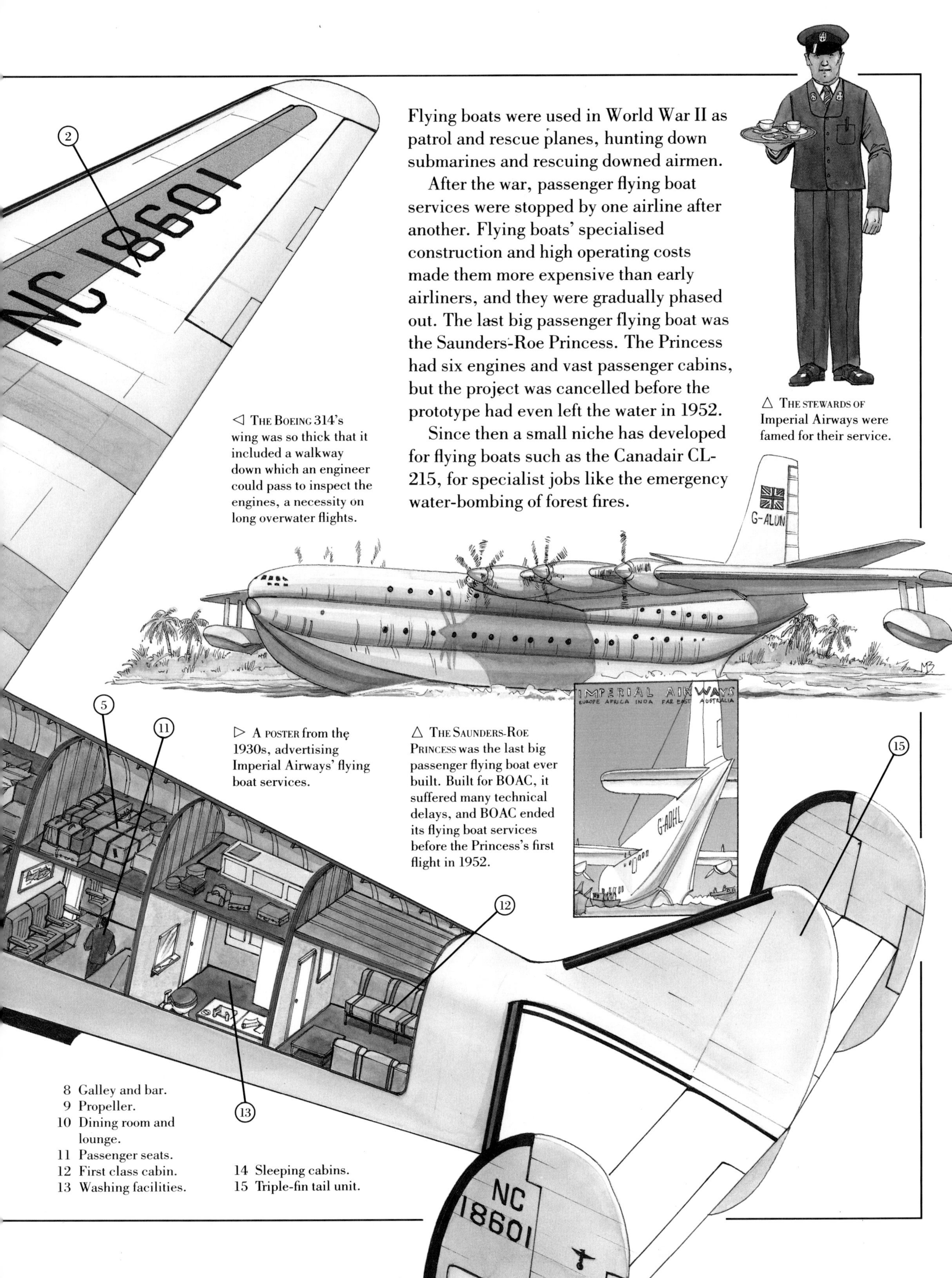

Flying boats were used in World War II as patrol and rescue planes, hunting down submarines and rescuing downed airmen.

After the war, passenger flying boat services were stopped by one airline after another. Flying boats' specialised construction and high operating costs made them more expensive than early airliners, and they were gradually phased out. The last big passenger flying boat was the Saunders-Roe Princess. The Princess had six engines and vast passenger cabins, but the project was cancelled before the prototype had even left the water in 1952.

Since then a small niche has developed for flying boats such as the Canadair CL-215, for specialist jobs like the emergency water-bombing of forest fires.

△ THE STEWARDS OF Imperial Airways were famed for their service.

◁ THE BOEING 314's wing was so thick that it included a walkway down which an engineer could pass to inspect the engines, a necessity on long overwater flights.

▷ A POSTER from the 1930s, advertising Imperial Airways' flying boat services.

△ THE SAUNDERS-ROE PRINCESS was the last big passenger flying boat ever built. Built for BOAC, it suffered many technical delays, and BOAC ended its flying boat services before the Princess's first flight in 1952.

8 Galley and bar.
9 Propeller.
10 Dining room and lounge.
11 Passenger seats.
12 First class cabin.
13 Washing facilities.
14 Sleeping cabins.
15 Triple-fin tail unit.

First Airliners

COMMERCIAL AVIATION MADE A FLYING START after World War I. The first airliners were based on bombers, with people in place of bombs. The Vickers Vimy Commercial included the first toilet for the comfort of its ten passengers. Bad weather was a danger for early aviators. The aircraft flew quite low, so were prey to the worst weather. The creation of air lanes was the result of a collision in cloud between two airliners in April 1922.

△ THE SIKORSKY S-38 was an amphibious craft. Though it had a flying boat hull, a retractable undercarriage allowed it to operate from airstrips. Pan American Airways flew S-38s from October 1928 on services to the Caribbean and South America.

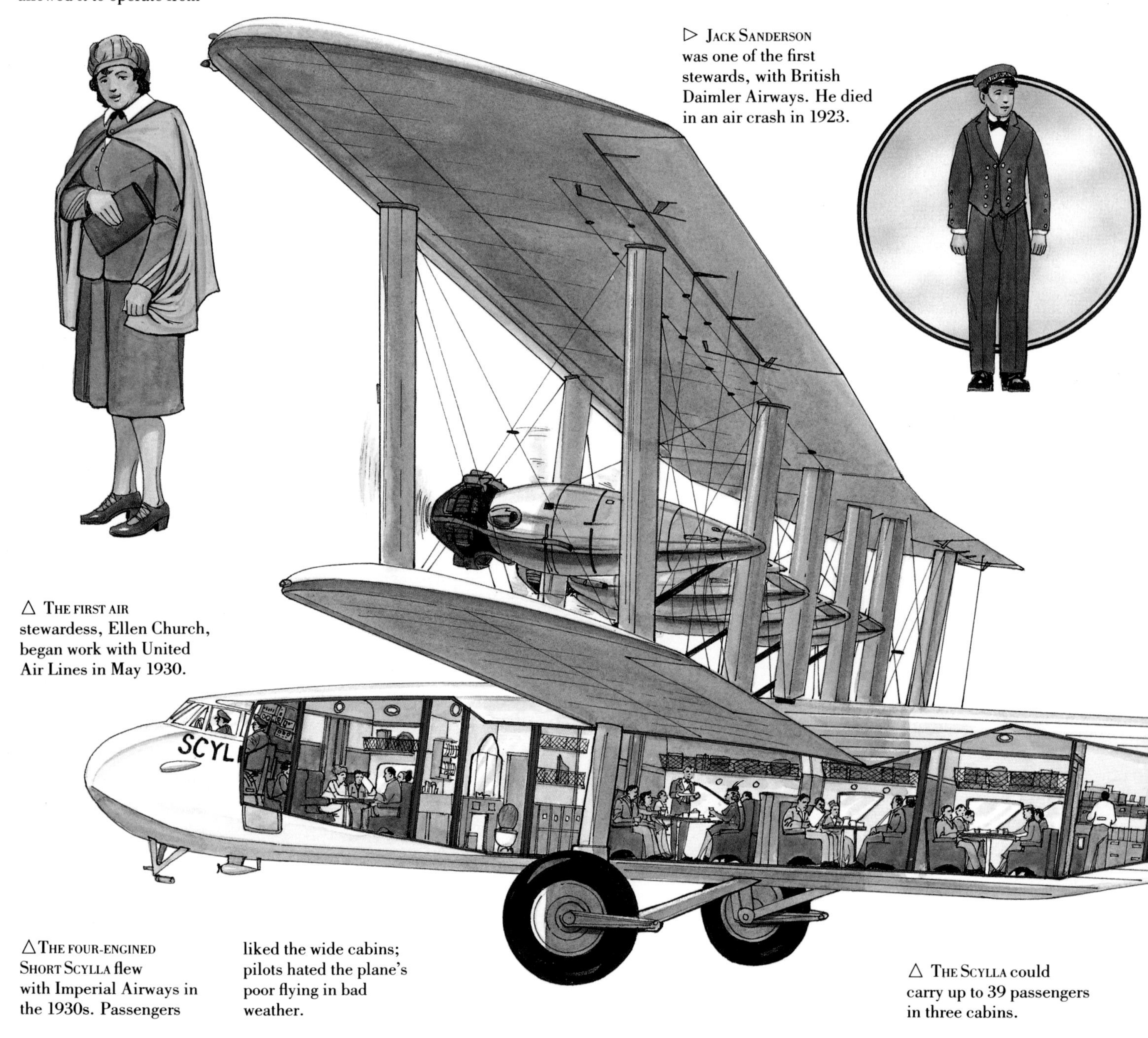

▷ JACK SANDERSON was one of the first stewards, with British Daimler Airways. He died in an air crash in 1923.

△ THE FIRST AIR stewardess, Ellen Church, began work with United Air Lines in May 1930.

△ THE FOUR-ENGINED SHORT SCYLLA flew with Imperial Airways in the 1930s. Passengers liked the wide cabins; pilots hated the plane's poor flying in bad weather.

△ THE SCYLLA could carry up to 39 passengers in three cabins.

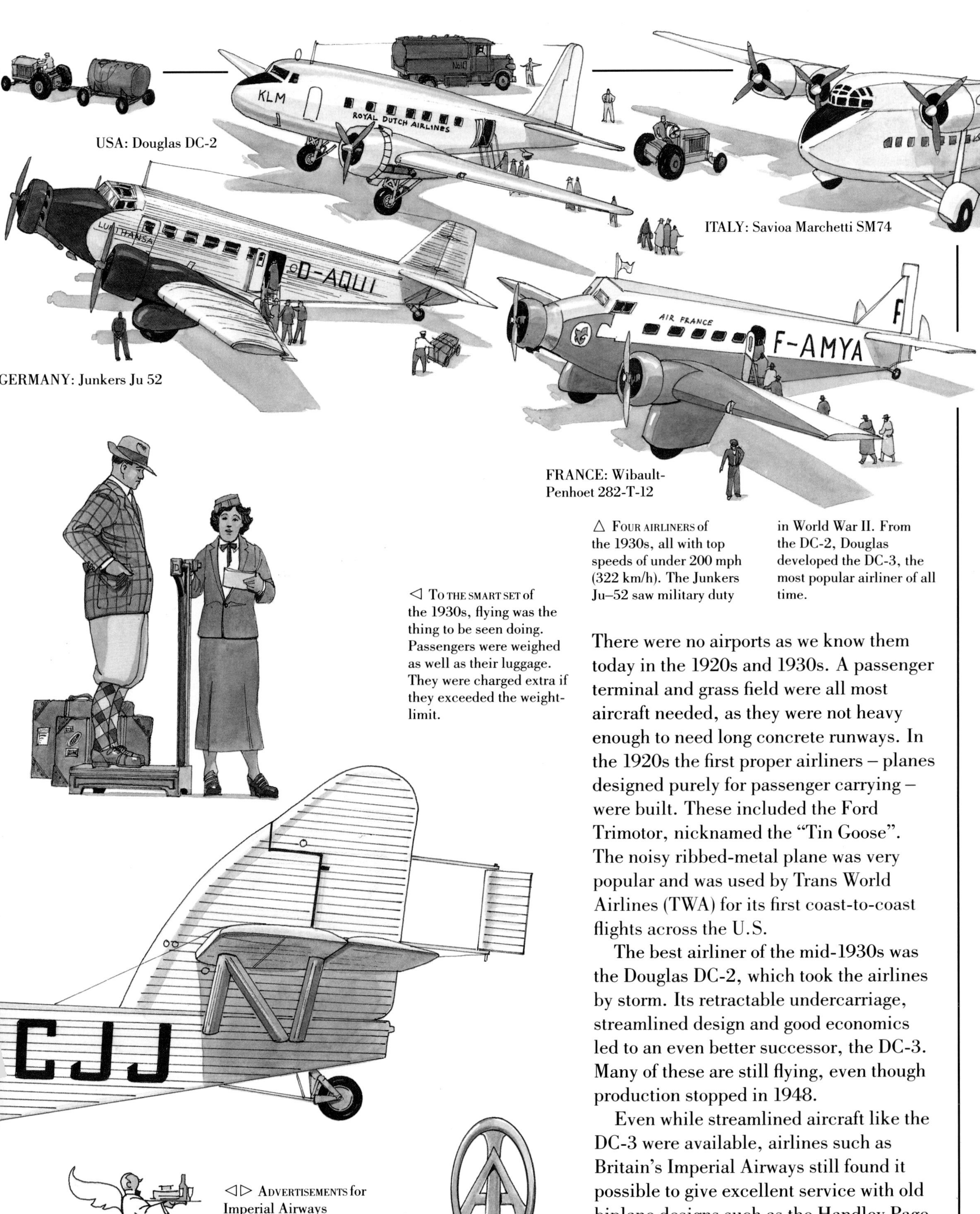

USA: Douglas DC-2

ITALY: Savioa Marchetti SM74

GERMANY: Junkers Ju 52

FRANCE: Wibault-Penhoet 282-T-12

△ FOUR AIRLINERS of the 1930s, all with top speeds of under 200 mph (322 km/h). The Junkers Ju–52 saw military duty in World War II. From the DC-2, Douglas developed the DC-3, the most popular airliner of all time.

◁ TO THE SMART SET of the 1930s, flying was the thing to be seen doing. Passengers were weighed as well as their luggage. They were charged extra if they exceeded the weight-limit.

There were no airports as we know them today in the 1920s and 1930s. A passenger terminal and grass field were all most aircraft needed, as they were not heavy enough to need long concrete runways. In the 1920s the first proper airliners – planes designed purely for passenger carrying – were built. These included the Ford Trimotor, nicknamed the "Tin Goose". The noisy ribbed-metal plane was very popular and was used by Trans World Airlines (TWA) for its first coast-to-coast flights across the U.S.

The best airliner of the mid-1930s was the Douglas DC-2, which took the airlines by storm. Its retractable undercarriage, streamlined design and good economics led to an even better successor, the DC-3. Many of these are still flying, even though production stopped in 1948.

Even while streamlined aircraft like the DC-3 were available, airlines such as Britain's Imperial Airways still found it possible to give excellent service with old biplane designs such as the Handley Page 42 and the Short Scylla shown left.

◁▷ ADVERTISEMENTS for Imperial Airways included these symbols of service and safety.

△ THE HAWKER HURRICANE PROVIDED the backbone of Britain's air defense.

▽ THE "WINGS" BADGE of the Royal Air Force.

▽ AIR FORCE CREWS were generally young men. The U.S. Air Force carried out daylight raids, the RAF bombed at night.

△ DORNIER DO-17 bombers were a standard German attack weapon.

THE ALLIES

WORLD WAR II INVOLVED massive land, sea and air battles across much of the world. Germany, Italy and Japan were known as the axis powers, while allied defenses were spearheaded by Britain, Russia, and the U.S.

When the war started, a new generation of fighters was coming into frontline squadron service, including aircraft such as the British Spitfire and Hurricane. Streamlined, all-metal monoplanes, they were armed with eight machine guns and had top speeds of 300 miles per hour (483 km/h) or more.

Despite the high speeds the new aircraft could achieve, air combats closely resembled those of World War I, with very similar combat maneuvers. Classic attack techniques, such as diving "out of the sun" to avoid being seen against the glare, were still winning moves. And whichever pilot had the faster or more agile aircraft had the advantage.

One thing had changed for the better though – allied pilots were issued parachutes, with rescue services to back them up. Training pilots to fly the expensive new aircraft took time and money, and pilots were too valuable to throw away.

▷ THE P-51D MUSTANG provided long-range escort protection to bomber groups.

△ MEMPHIS BELLE was one of the most famous B-17s. This badge was painted on the nose.

Major air conflicts included the Battle of Britain in 1940. Only newly-developed radar warning systems enabled Spitfires and Hurricanes to be in the air at the right time and place to engage German forces.

Later in the war, allied forces started huge bombing campaigns. In daylight, American aircraft such as the Boeing B-17 were used. At night, British bombers such as the Avro Lancaster attacked factories, dams and other targets.

The last major attacks of the war were also bombing missions. In August 1945, atomic bombs destroyed the Japanese cities of Hiroshima and Nagasaki.

△ One of the best fighters of the war was the Vickers-Supermarine Spitfire. Early versions were armed with eight machine guns. Later, cannon were added to the plane's armory.

△ The most important items in this RAF pilot's outfit were an oxygen mask for battle at high altitude, a parachute to escape a damaged plane and a life jacket to survive a ditching in the sea.

△ The Avro Lancaster was the RAF's best heavy bomber. It could carry a range of weapons, including the massive 10-ton Grand Slam bomb.

▽ The Boeing B-17 was named the Flying Fortress, for its defenses of up to a dozen machine guns. The B-17 could cruise at 160 mph (258 km/h), carrying a bomb load of nearly two tons.

△ The four-engined Boeing B-17 was one of the main Allied daylight bombers.

Axis Powers

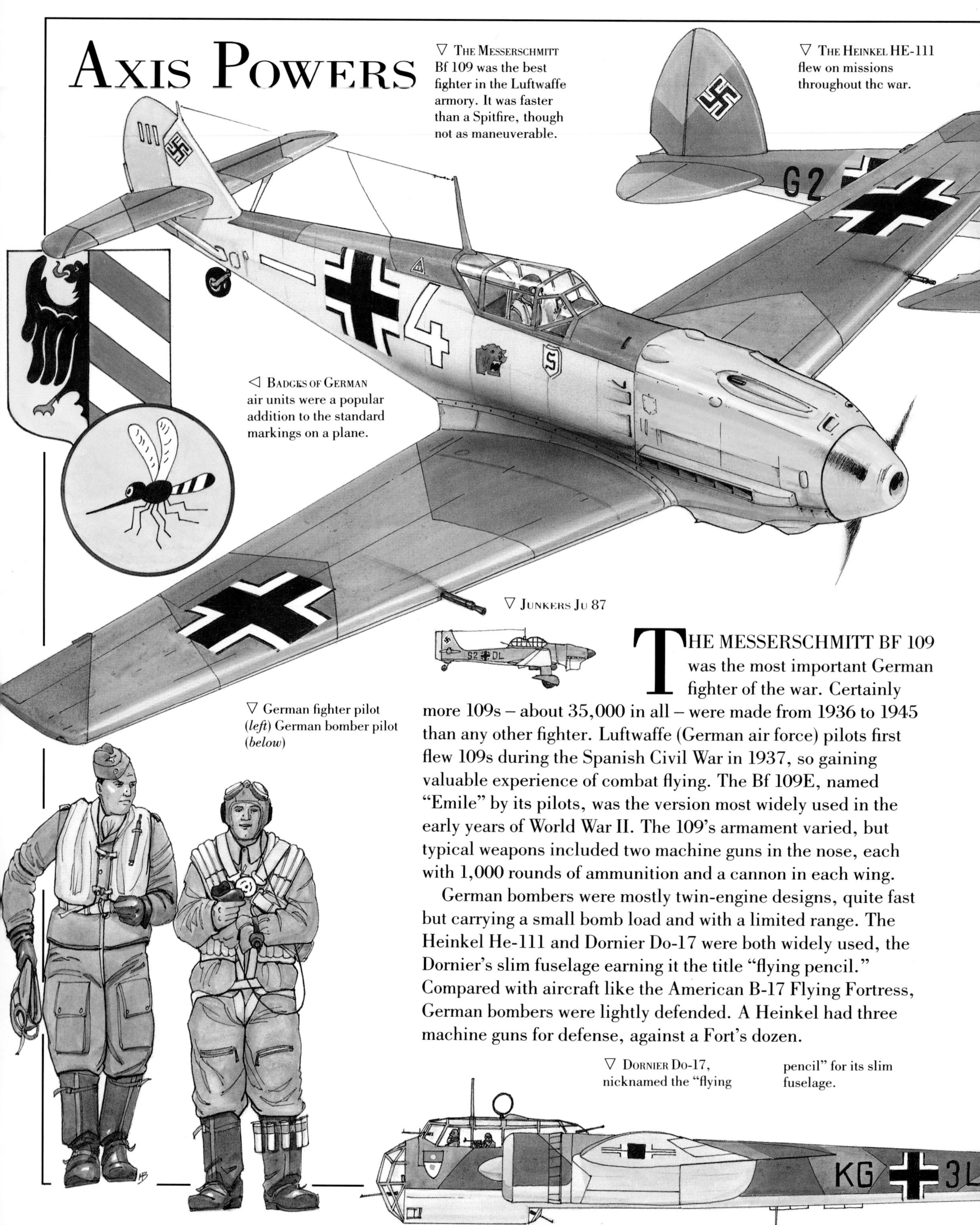

▽ The Messerschmitt Bf 109 was the best fighter in the Luftwaffe armory. It was faster than a Spitfire, though not as maneuverable.

▽ The Heinkel HE-111 flew on missions throughout the war.

◁ Badges of German air units were a popular addition to the standard markings on a plane.

▽ Junkers Ju 87

▽ German fighter pilot (*left*) German bomber pilot (*below*)

THE MESSERSCHMITT BF 109 was the most important German fighter of the war. Certainly more 109s – about 35,000 in all – were made from 1936 to 1945 than any other fighter. Luftwaffe (German air force) pilots first flew 109s during the Spanish Civil War in 1937, so gaining valuable experience of combat flying. The Bf 109E, named "Emile" by its pilots, was the version most widely used in the early years of World War II. The 109's armament varied, but typical weapons included two machine guns in the nose, each with 1,000 rounds of ammunition and a cannon in each wing.

German bombers were mostly twin-engine designs, quite fast but carrying a small bomb load and with a limited range. The Heinkel He-111 and Dornier Do-17 were both widely used, the Dornier's slim fuselage earning it the title "flying pencil." Compared with aircraft like the American B-17 Flying Fortress, German bombers were lightly defended. A Heinkel had three machine guns for defense, against a Fort's dozen.

▽ Dornier Do-17, nicknamed the "flying pencil" for its slim fuselage.

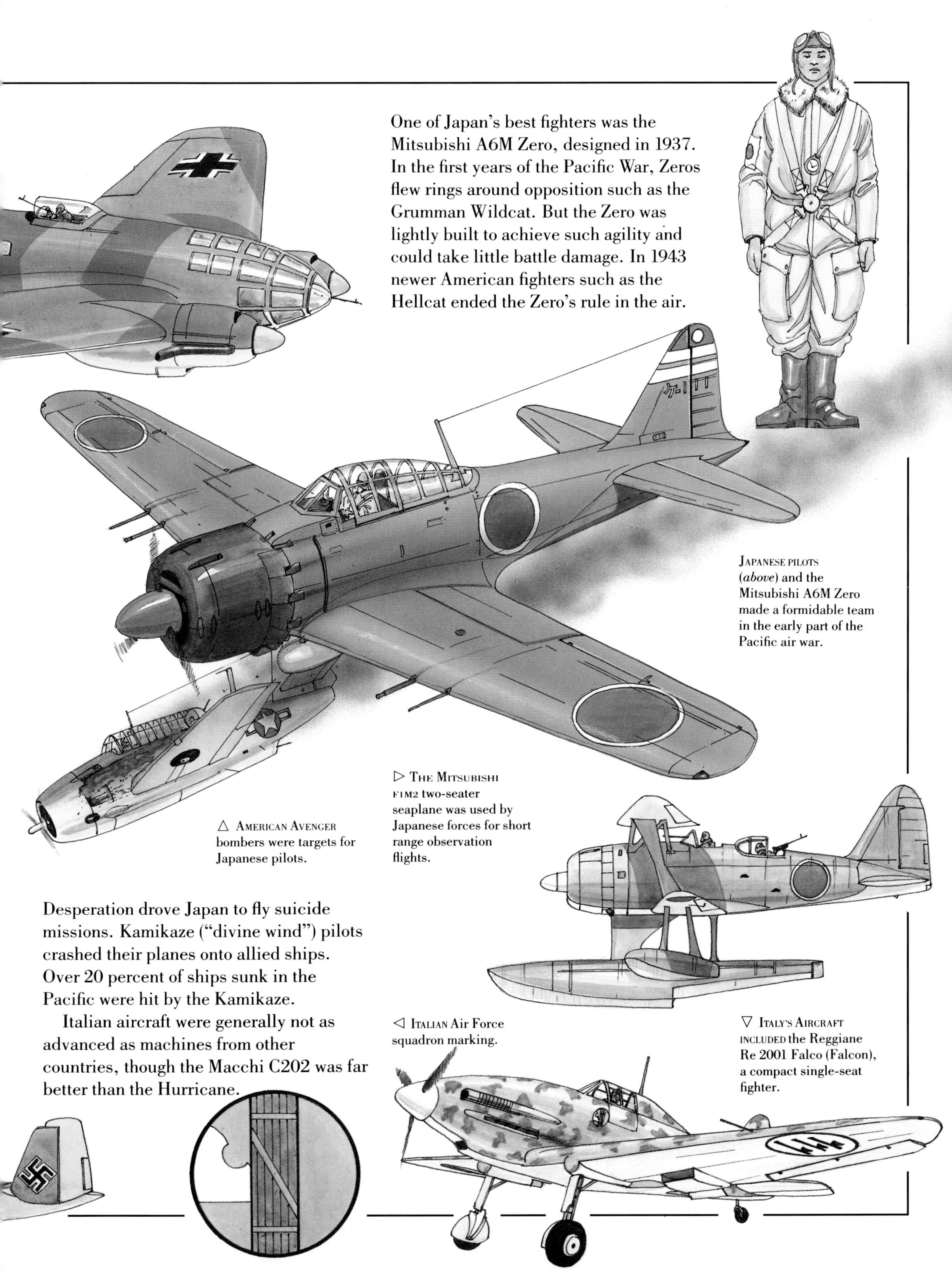

One of Japan's best fighters was the Mitsubishi A6M Zero, designed in 1937. In the first years of the Pacific War, Zeros flew rings around opposition such as the Grumman Wildcat. But the Zero was lightly built to achieve such agility and could take little battle damage. In 1943 newer American fighters such as the Hellcat ended the Zero's rule in the air.

JAPANESE PILOTS (*above*) and the Mitsubishi A6M Zero made a formidable team in the early part of the Pacific air war.

△ AMERICAN AVENGER bombers were targets for Japanese pilots.

▷ THE MITSUBISHI F1M2 two-seater seaplane was used by Japanese forces for short range observation flights.

Desperation drove Japan to fly suicide missions. Kamikaze ("divine wind") pilots crashed their planes onto allied ships. Over 20 percent of ships sunk in the Pacific were hit by the Kamikaze.

Italian aircraft were generally not as advanced as machines from other countries, though the Macchi C202 was far better than the Hurricane.

◁ ITALIAN Air Force squadron marking.

▽ ITALY'S AIRCRAFT INCLUDED the Reggiane Re 2001 Falco (Falcon), a compact single-seat fighter.

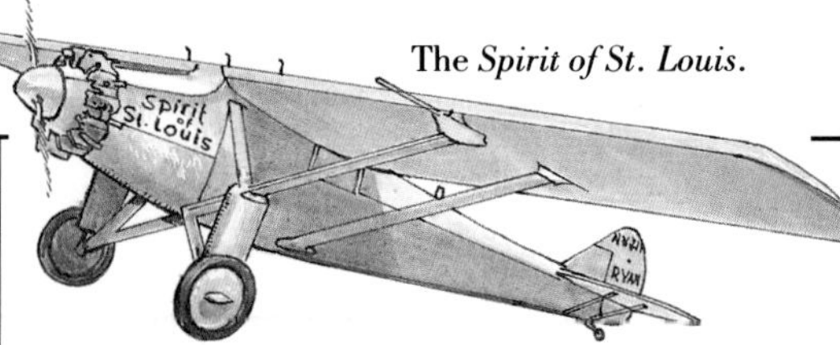

The *Spirit of St. Louis*.

EPIC FLIGHTS

THE STORY OF AVIATION HAS BEEN THAT of flying faster, higher and farther than anyone else. Before World War II, the main aim was to conquer distance, proving routes suitable for airmail and passenger flights.

The Atlantic was first flown nonstop by two British fliers, John Alcock and Arthur Brown in 1919. They flew a Vickers Vimy bomber, with fuel instead of weapons. It was not until 1927 that a solo flight was achieved. On May 21, Charles Lindbergh landed in Paris after over 33 hours in the air. By the 1980s few long-distance challenges were left, except around the world, unrefueled, accomplished by Dick Rutan and Jeana Yeager in 1986.

△ AMY JOHNSON made history by flying her de Havilland Gypsy Moth from England to Australia in 1930.

▽ Names of some important record breaking aircraft. The globe shows their routes.

1 Douglas World Cruiser
2 Curtiss NC-4
3 Vickers Vimy
4 Latecoere 28
5 *Spirit of St. Louis*
6 Ford Trimotor
7 Fokker FVII/3m
8 De Havilland Gypsy Moth
9 Lockheed Vega
10 Westland Wallace
11 Lockheed Electra
12 Boeing 247
13 Douglas DC-2
14 De Havilland DH88 Comet
15 Rutan *Voyager*

PANGBORN & HERNDON 1931
KINGSFORD-SMITH & ULM 1928
AMY JOHNSON 1930
POST & GATTY 1931
SCOTT & BLACK 1934
ALCOCK & BROWN 1919
LINDBERGH 1927
CABRAL & COUTUSHO 1922
NC4 1919

AFTER WORLD WAR I, aviators flew longer and longer flights around the world, paving the way for the scheduled airline flights to come.

THE JET AGE

△ THE GERMAN HEINKEL He-178 was the first jet to fly. It first took off in August 1939.

THE FIRST JET INTO THE AIR was a German Heinkel He-178. On August 27, 1939, Erich Warsitz piloted the small single-engine plane on a test circuit at Marienhe. The first jet in combat was German, too, in 1944. The Messerschmitt Me 262 was much faster than allied fighters such as the Mustang, but not enough were made to make much difference to the massed allied air raids which led to Germany's defeat.

The high speed of the new jets meant a fresh danger in the air. When aircraft tried to go faster than the speed of sound (about 760 miles per hour [1224 km/h] at sea level, slower at altitude) they were buffeted and pounded by severe shockwaves.

△ IN 1947, AMERICAN CHUCK YEAGER broke the "sound barrier" in the Bell X-1 rocket plane. Until then, many people had thought that the destructive shockwaves of very high speed flight were impossible to overcome.

△ ITALY'S BIG CAPRONI-CAMPINI CC1 flew in 1940, but did not prove a great success.

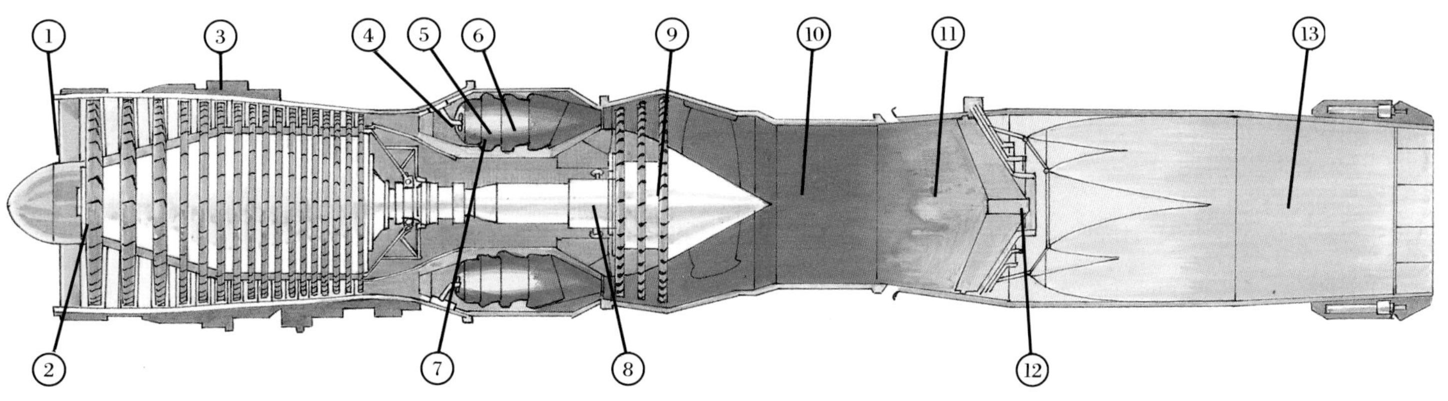

1 Air intake.
2 Compressor blades.
3 Metal casing.
4 Fuel injectors.
5 Combustion chamber.
6 Vaporized fuel.
7 Igniters.
8 Shaft joining compressor to turbine.
9 Rear turbine.
10 Hot gases.
11 Afterburner.
12 Fuel injectors.
13 Jet pipe.

◁ THE BRITISH GLOSTER E.28/39 first flew in 1941.

△ THE TWIN-ENGINED BELL XP-59A of 1942 was the first American jet.

These aircraft show how speeds have increased since the first flights of the Wright brothers.

A 1903 Wright Flyer 30 mph (48 km/h).
B 1912 Deperdussin Racer 130 mph (209 km/h).
C 1933 Northrop Gamma 157 mph (293 km/h).
D 1927 Ryan Spirit of St. Louis 124 mph (200 km/h).
E 1935 Douglas DC-3 210 mph (338 km/h).
F 1942 North American P-51D 437 mph (703 km/h)
G 1954 Boeing 707 620 mph (998 km/h).
H 1969 Aerospatiale Concorde 1,320 mph. (2125 km/h).
I 1962 Lockheed SR-71 over 2,000 mph (3220 km/h).

The "sound barrier" was thought to be impassable, until Chuck Yeager broke it in a Bell X-1 in 1947. This was a rocket plane, but the design principles required for supersonic flight applied to jet aircraft, too.

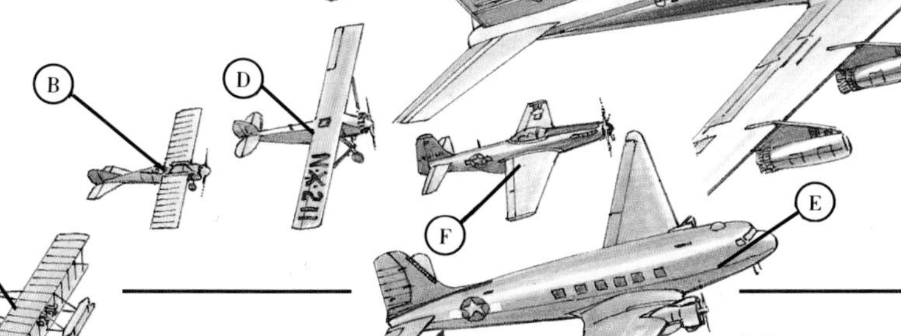

AIRPORTS

FAST, RELIABLE JET AIRLINERS such as the Boeing 707 (*right*) and Douglas DC-8 led to a massive growth in civil aviation in the 1960s. From being an expensive luxury for the rich, airline flying became the easiest and cheapest way for nearly anyone. With the increase in passengers carried came the equal demands of handling the numbers on the ground. Airports all over the world built new terminals and extended their runways. The airport shown here is typical of the hugely expensive facilities required in the jetliner age.

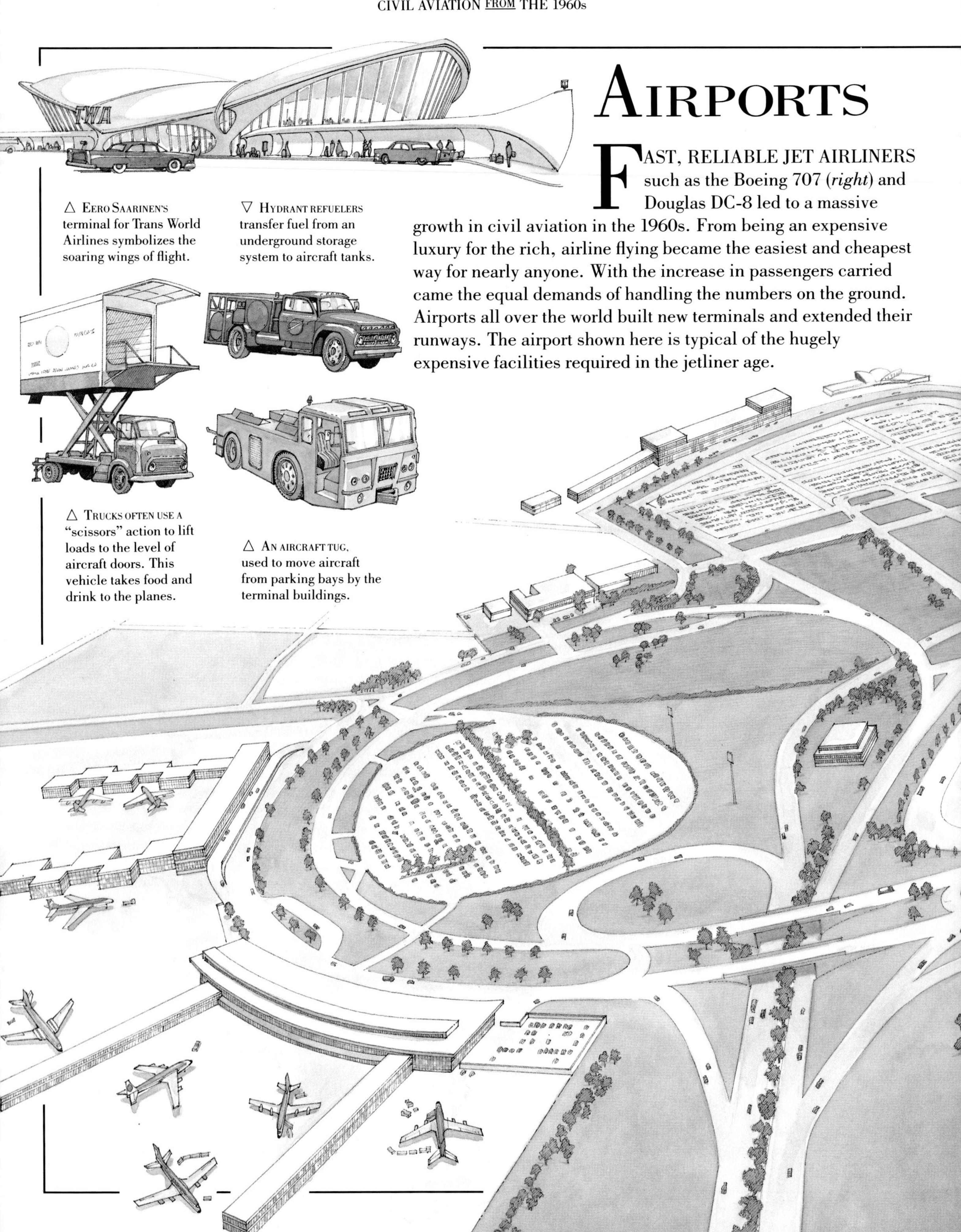

△ EERO SAARINEN'S terminal for Trans World Airlines symbolizes the soaring wings of flight.

▽ HYDRANT REFUELERS transfer fuel from an underground storage system to aircraft tanks.

△ TRUCKS OFTEN USE A "scissors" action to lift loads to the level of aircraft doors. This vehicle takes food and drink to the planes.

△ AN AIRCRAFT TUG, used to move aircraft from parking bays by the terminal buildings.

▽ The control tower (*below*) is the nerve center of any airport. From here ground controllers direct all aircraft to and from runways and when parking.

Approach and departure controllers direct the flights as they take off and land. Powerful radars sweep the skies to give tower staff a complete picture of air traffic around the airport.

If the first jetliners created an air travel revolution then the advent of the mighty Boeing 747 of 1969 repeated the process. Able to carry a load of 375 or more passengers, the 747 made flying as cheap as using a private car. The extra passengers forced airports to grow all over again, an expansion still going on.

Airports handle freight as well as passengers, ranging from livestock to diamonds. Freight is carried both on specialist cargo planes and in metal containers carried under airliner passenger decks. One airport alone, London's Heathrow, handles over 500,000 tons of freight a year. Large airports such as these are like small cities: some 50,000 people depend on Heathrow for a living. Their jobs range from cooks and cleaners to customs officers and security staff.

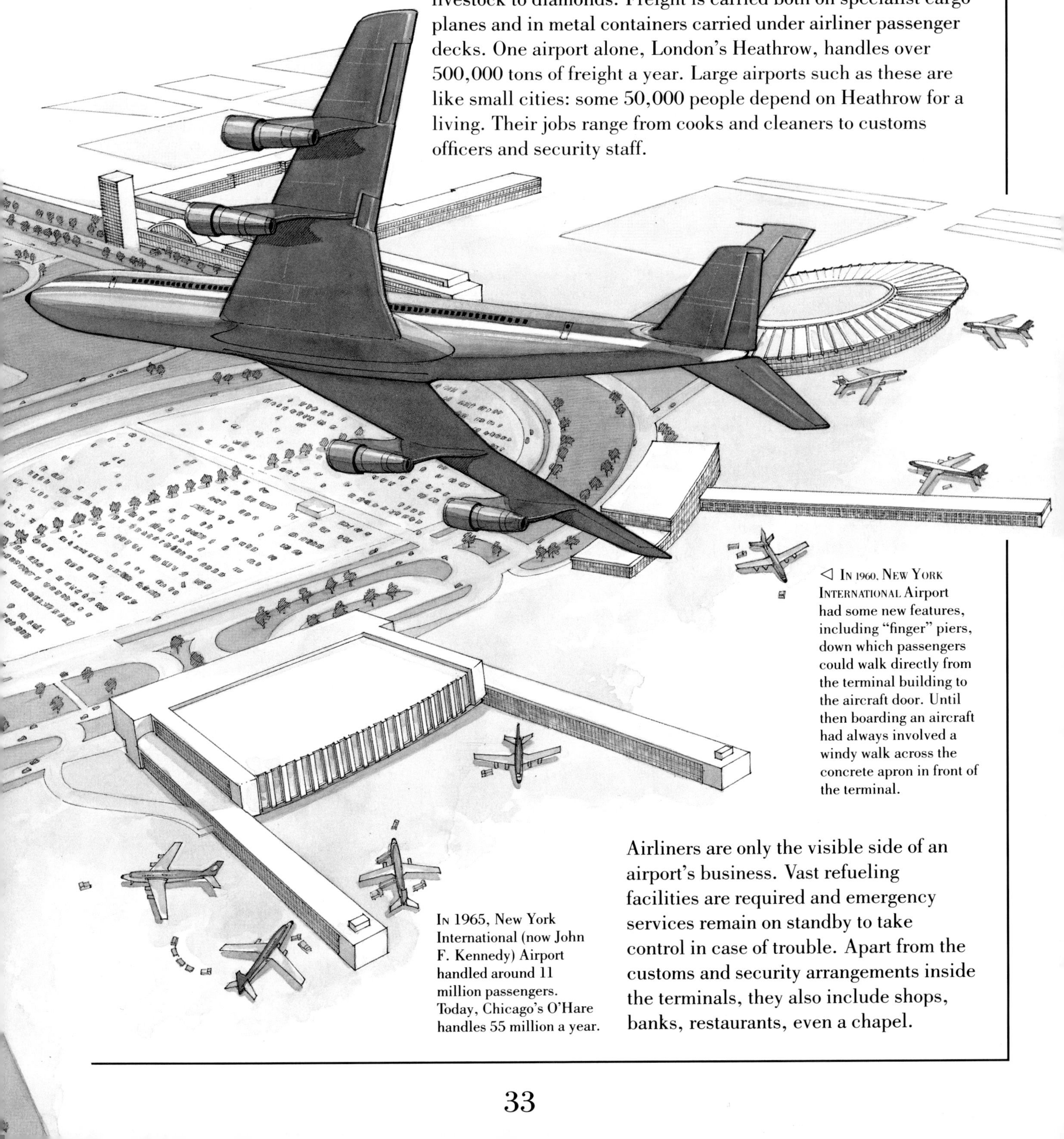

◁ In 1960, New York International Airport had some new features, including "finger" piers, down which passengers could walk directly from the terminal building to the aircraft door. Until then boarding an aircraft had always involved a windy walk across the concrete apron in front of the terminal.

In 1965, New York International (now John F. Kennedy) Airport handled around 11 million passengers. Today, Chicago's O'Hare handles 55 million a year.

Airliners are only the visible side of an airport's business. Vast refueling facilities are required and emergency services remain on standby to take control in case of trouble. Apart from the customs and security arrangements inside the terminals, they also include shops, banks, restaurants, even a chapel.

△ CONCORDE, still the only supersonic airliner.

AIRLINERS

THE WORLD'S FIRST SUPERSONIC AIRLINER was created by teams from France and Britain. Concorde's maiden flight was on March 2, 1969, and planners dreamed of Concorde fleets with all major airlines. It was not to be. Fuel prices skyrocketed in the 1970s, making Concorde's high running costs too expensive for most airlines.

Today, only British Airways and Air France operate small numbers of these airliners, offering a premium service to high-spending travelers. In return for top price air fares, Concorde passengers have their own check-in facilities and a quality of service not seen since the flying boat days of the 1930s.

As modern airliners go, the Concorde is on the small side, seating about 128 passengers. In the front of the cabin, a digital display shows the aircraft's speed: Mach 1 as it passes through the sound barrier, Mach 2 as it settles down to fly at around 1,320 miles per hour (2125 km/h). Concorde's cruising altitude, at 60,000 feet (18300 m) is far above other airliners.

△ CONCORDE'S FLIGHT DECK is old-fashioned by 1990s standards. Today's more modern aircraft have had the old mechanical instruments replaced with computer-controlled digital TV displays.

If Concorde is a slim, expensive-to-fly luxury, then the aircraft built by Airbus Industrie are the exact opposite. Dating from the 1960s, Airbus Industrie is a group of makers from Europe, led by the French firm Aerospatiale. The first Airbus design, the A-300 (opposite), flew within months of Concorde's first flight. The A-300 was to provide cheap flying costs in a high tech, though ordinary looking, package. The plane has been a major success, and 20 years after its first flight, over 300 fly with the world's airlines.

▷ COLORFUL AIRLINE LUGGAGE LABELS from the 1950s and 1960s.

▽ CONCORDE'S NOSE SECTION droops on takeoff and landing, allowing the flight crew to see ahead, despite the plane's nose-high angle when flying slowly. At speed, the nose lifts and a windscreen cover slides into place.

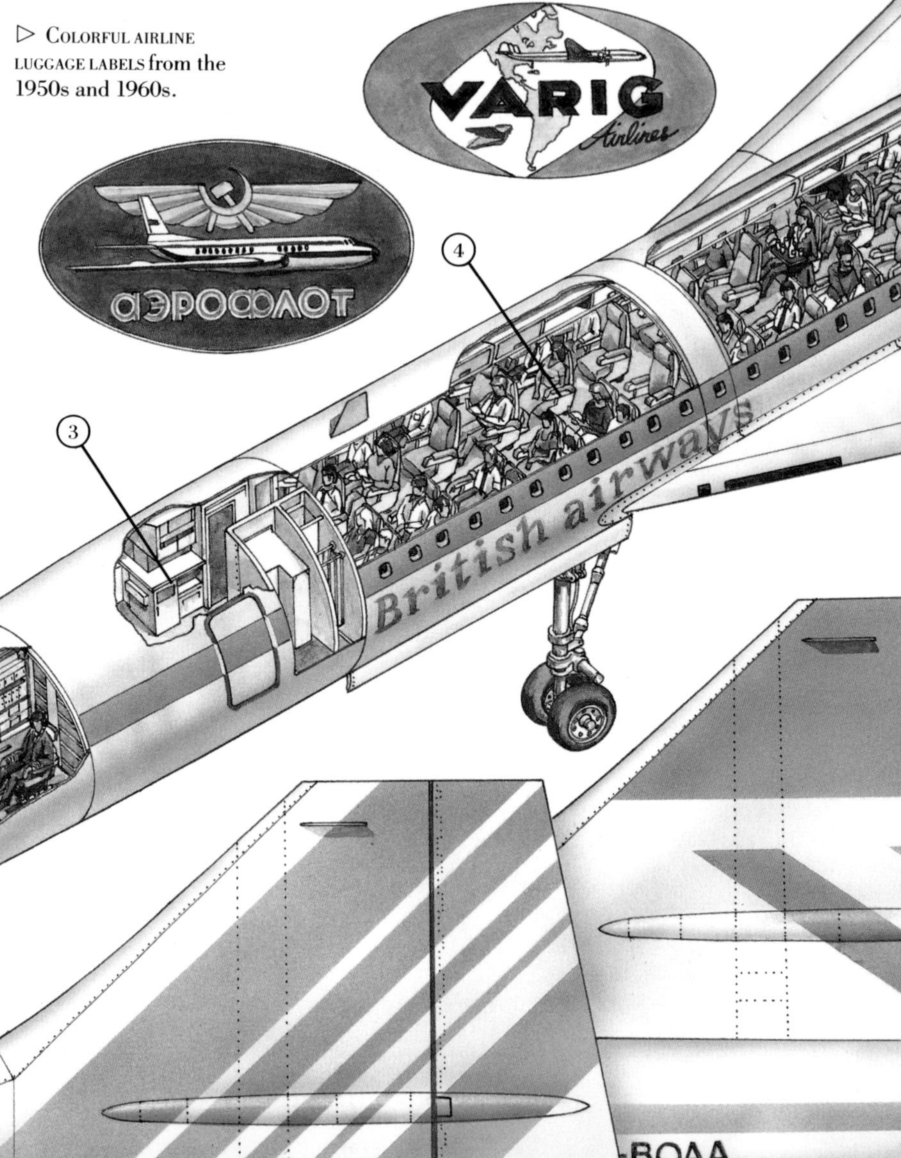

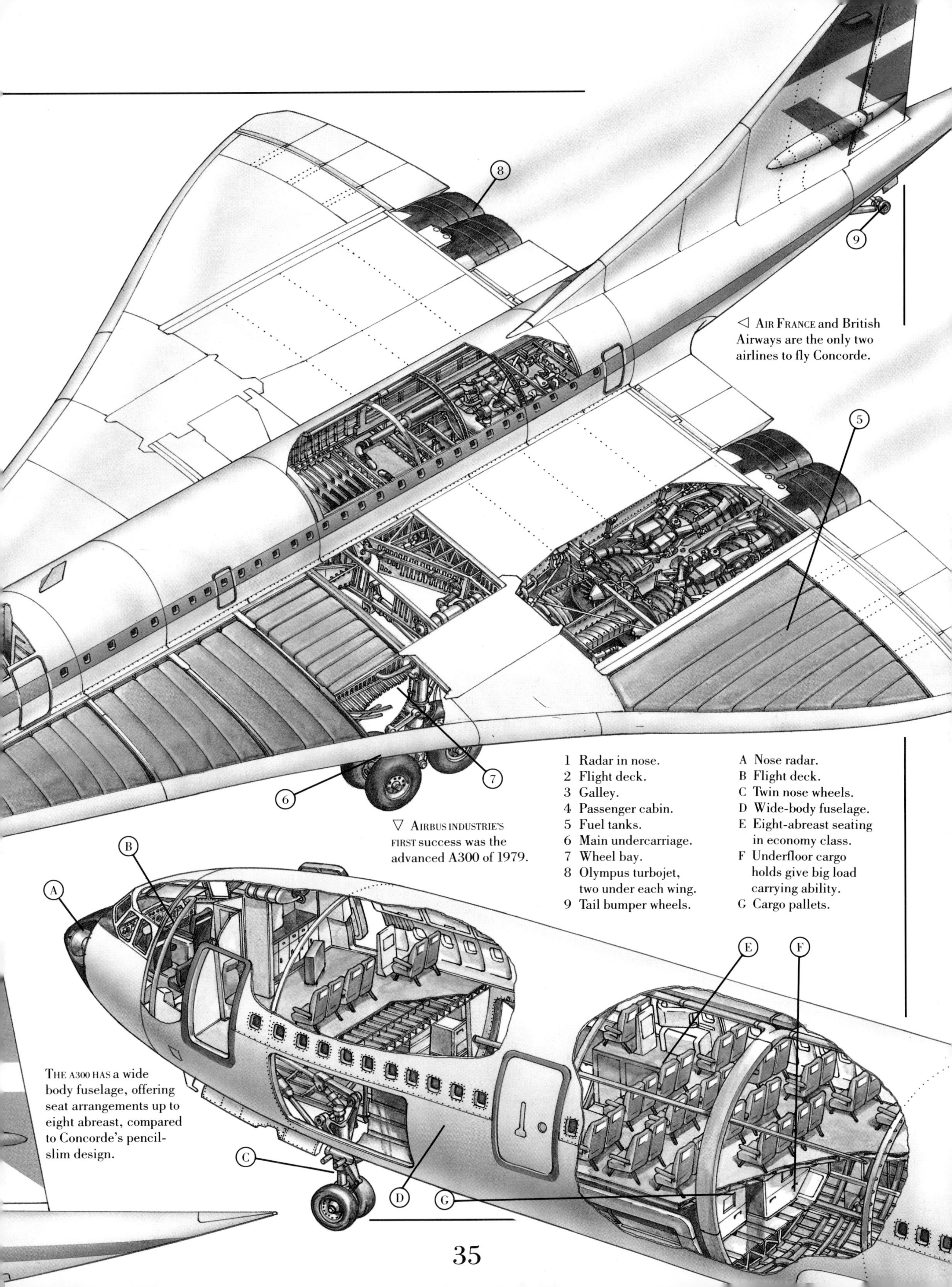

◁ AIR FRANCE and British Airways are the only two airlines to fly Concorde.

▽ AIRBUS INDUSTRIE'S FIRST success was the advanced A300 of 1979.

1 Radar in nose.
2 Flight deck.
3 Galley.
4 Passenger cabin.
5 Fuel tanks.
6 Main undercarriage.
7 Wheel bay.
8 Olympus turbojet, two under each wing.
9 Tail bumper wheels.

A Nose radar.
B Flight deck.
C Twin nose wheels.
D Wide-body fuselage.
E Eight-abreast seating in economy class.
F Underfloor cargo holds give big load carrying ability.
G Cargo pallets.

THE A300 HAS a wide body fuselage, offering seat arrangements up to eight abreast, compared to Concorde's pencil-slim design.

HELICOPTERS

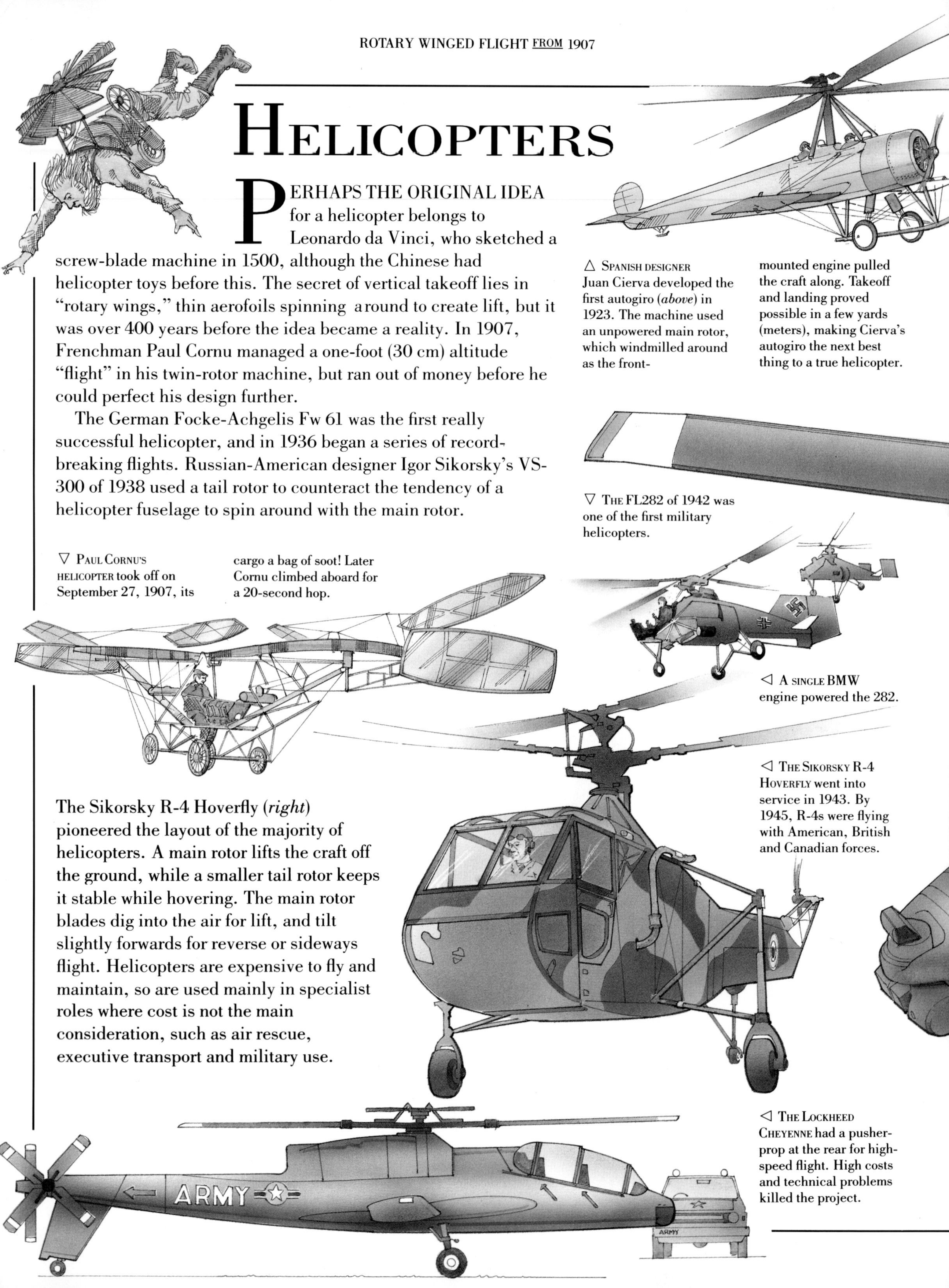

PERHAPS THE ORIGINAL IDEA for a helicopter belongs to Leonardo da Vinci, who sketched a screw-blade machine in 1500, although the Chinese had helicopter toys before this. The secret of vertical takeoff lies in "rotary wings," thin aerofoils spinning around to create lift, but it was over 400 years before the idea became a reality. In 1907, Frenchman Paul Cornu managed a one-foot (30 cm) altitude "flight" in his twin-rotor machine, but ran out of money before he could perfect his design further.

The German Focke-Achgelis Fw 61 was the first really successful helicopter, and in 1936 began a series of record-breaking flights. Russian-American designer Igor Sikorsky's VS-300 of 1938 used a tail rotor to counteract the tendency of a helicopter fuselage to spin around with the main rotor.

△ SPANISH DESIGNER Juan Cierva developed the first autogiro (*above*) in 1923. The machine used an unpowered main rotor, which windmilled around as the front-mounted engine pulled the craft along. Takeoff and landing proved possible in a few yards (meters), making Cierva's autogiro the next best thing to a true helicopter.

▽ THE FL282 of 1942 was one of the first military helicopters.

◁ A SINGLE BMW engine powered the 282.

▽ PAUL CORNU'S HELICOPTER took off on September 27, 1907, its cargo a bag of soot! Later Cornu climbed aboard for a 20-second hop.

The Sikorsky R-4 Hoverfly (*right*) pioneered the layout of the majority of helicopters. A main rotor lifts the craft off the ground, while a smaller tail rotor keeps it stable while hovering. The main rotor blades dig into the air for lift, and tilt slightly forwards for reverse or sideways flight. Helicopters are expensive to fly and maintain, so are used mainly in specialist roles where cost is not the main consideration, such as air rescue, executive transport and military use.

◁ THE SIKORSKY R-4 HOVERFLY went into service in 1943. By 1945, R-4s were flying with American, British and Canadian forces.

◁ THE LOCKHEED CHEYENNE had a pusher-prop at the rear for high-speed flight. High costs and technical problems killed the project.

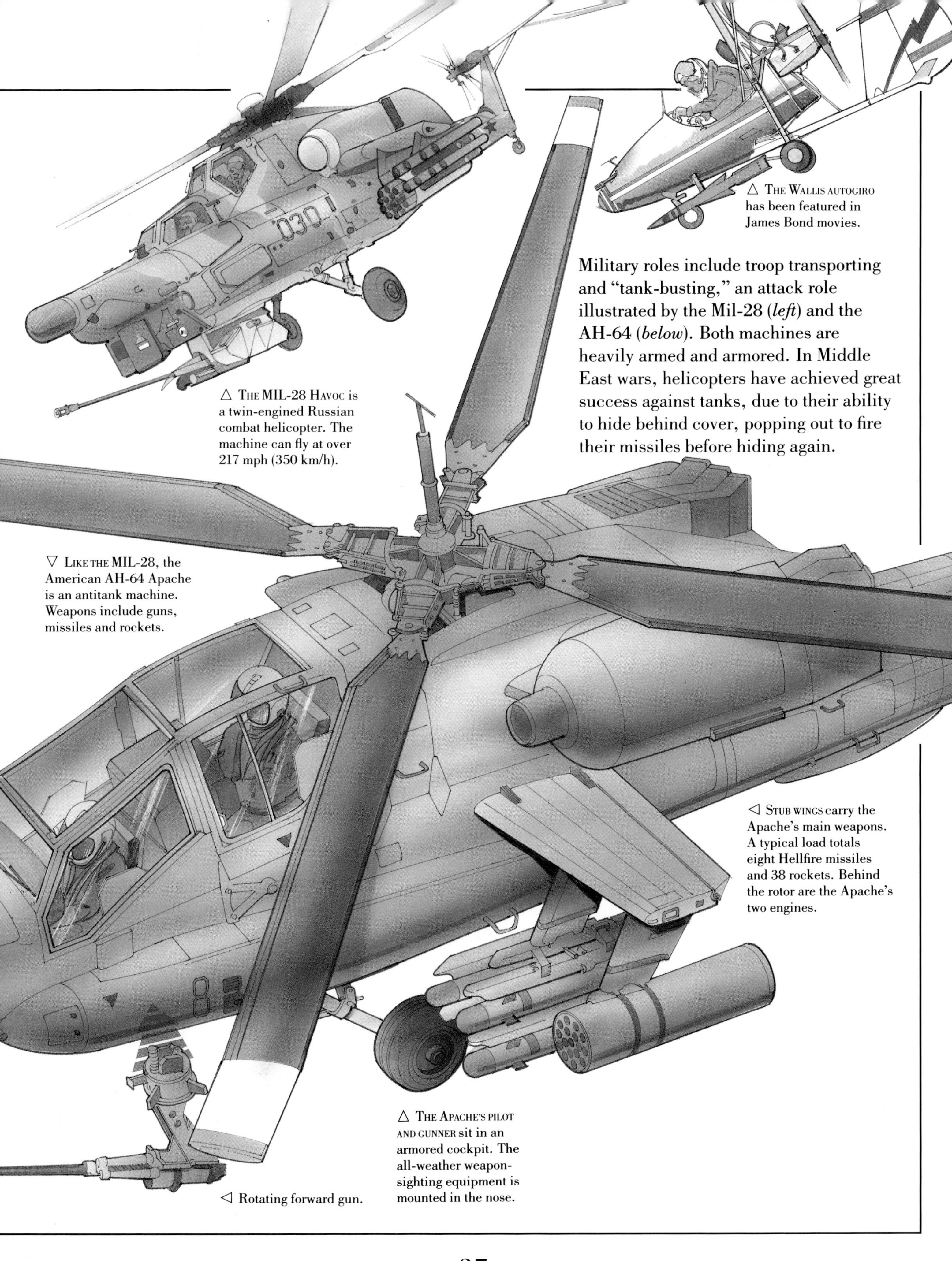

△ The Wallis autogiro has been featured in James Bond movies.

Military roles include troop transporting and "tank-busting," an attack role illustrated by the Mil-28 (*left*) and the AH-64 (*below*). Both machines are heavily armed and armored. In Middle East wars, helicopters have achieved great success against tanks, due to their ability to hide behind cover, popping out to fire their missiles before hiding again.

△ The MIL-28 Havoc is a twin-engined Russian combat helicopter. The machine can fly at over 217 mph (350 km/h).

▽ Like the MIL-28, the American AH-64 Apache is an antitank machine. Weapons include guns, missiles and rockets.

◁ Stub wings carry the Apache's main weapons. A typical load totals eight Hellfire missiles and 38 rockets. Behind the rotor are the Apache's two engines.

◁ Rotating forward gun.

△ The Apache's pilot and gunner sit in an armored cockpit. The all-weather weapon-sighting equipment is mounted in the nose.

General Aviation

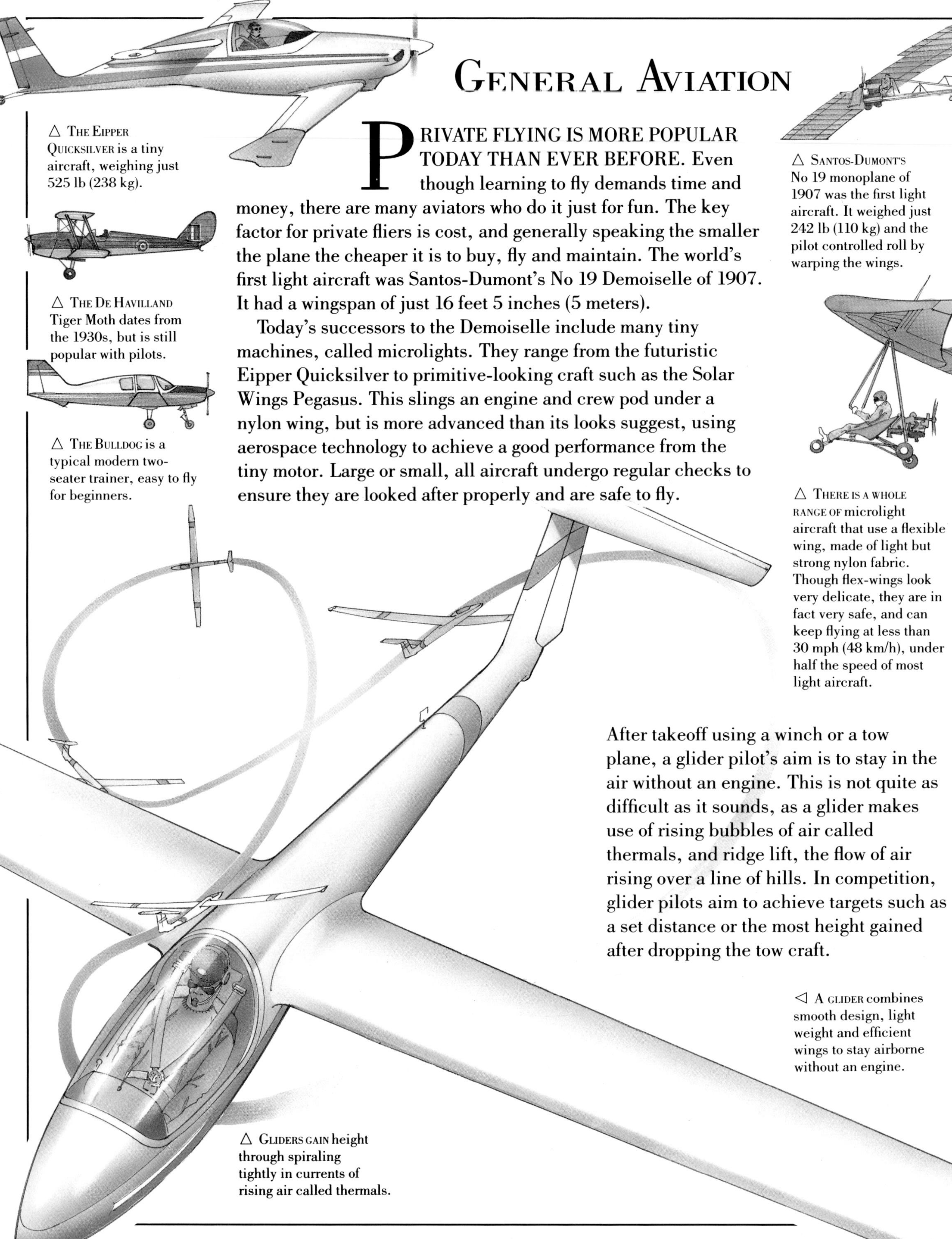

PRIVATE FLYING IS MORE POPULAR TODAY THAN EVER BEFORE. Even though learning to fly demands time and money, there are many aviators who do it just for fun. The key factor for private fliers is cost, and generally speaking the smaller the plane the cheaper it is to buy, fly and maintain. The world's first light aircraft was Santos-Dumont's No 19 Demoiselle of 1907. It had a wingspan of just 16 feet 5 inches (5 meters).

Today's successors to the Demoiselle include many tiny machines, called microlights. They range from the futuristic Eipper Quicksilver to primitive-looking craft such as the Solar Wings Pegasus. This slings an engine and crew pod under a nylon wing, but is more advanced than its looks suggest, using aerospace technology to achieve a good performance from the tiny motor. Large or small, all aircraft undergo regular checks to ensure they are looked after properly and are safe to fly.

△ The Eipper Quicksilver is a tiny aircraft, weighing just 525 lb (238 kg).

△ The De Havilland Tiger Moth dates from the 1930s, but is still popular with pilots.

△ The Bulldog is a typical modern two-seater trainer, easy to fly for beginners.

△ Santos-Dumont's No 19 monoplane of 1907 was the first light aircraft. It weighed just 242 lb (110 kg) and the pilot controlled roll by warping the wings.

△ There is a whole range of microlight aircraft that use a flexible wing, made of light but strong nylon fabric. Though flex-wings look very delicate, they are in fact very safe, and can keep flying at less than 30 mph (48 km/h), under half the speed of most light aircraft.

After takeoff using a winch or a tow plane, a glider pilot's aim is to stay in the air without an engine. This is not quite as difficult as it sounds, as a glider makes use of rising bubbles of air called thermals, and ridge lift, the flow of air rising over a line of hills. In competition, glider pilots aim to achieve targets such as a set distance or the most height gained after dropping the tow craft.

◁ A glider combines smooth design, light weight and efficient wings to stay airborne without an engine.

△ Gliders gain height through spiraling tightly in currents of rising air called thermals.

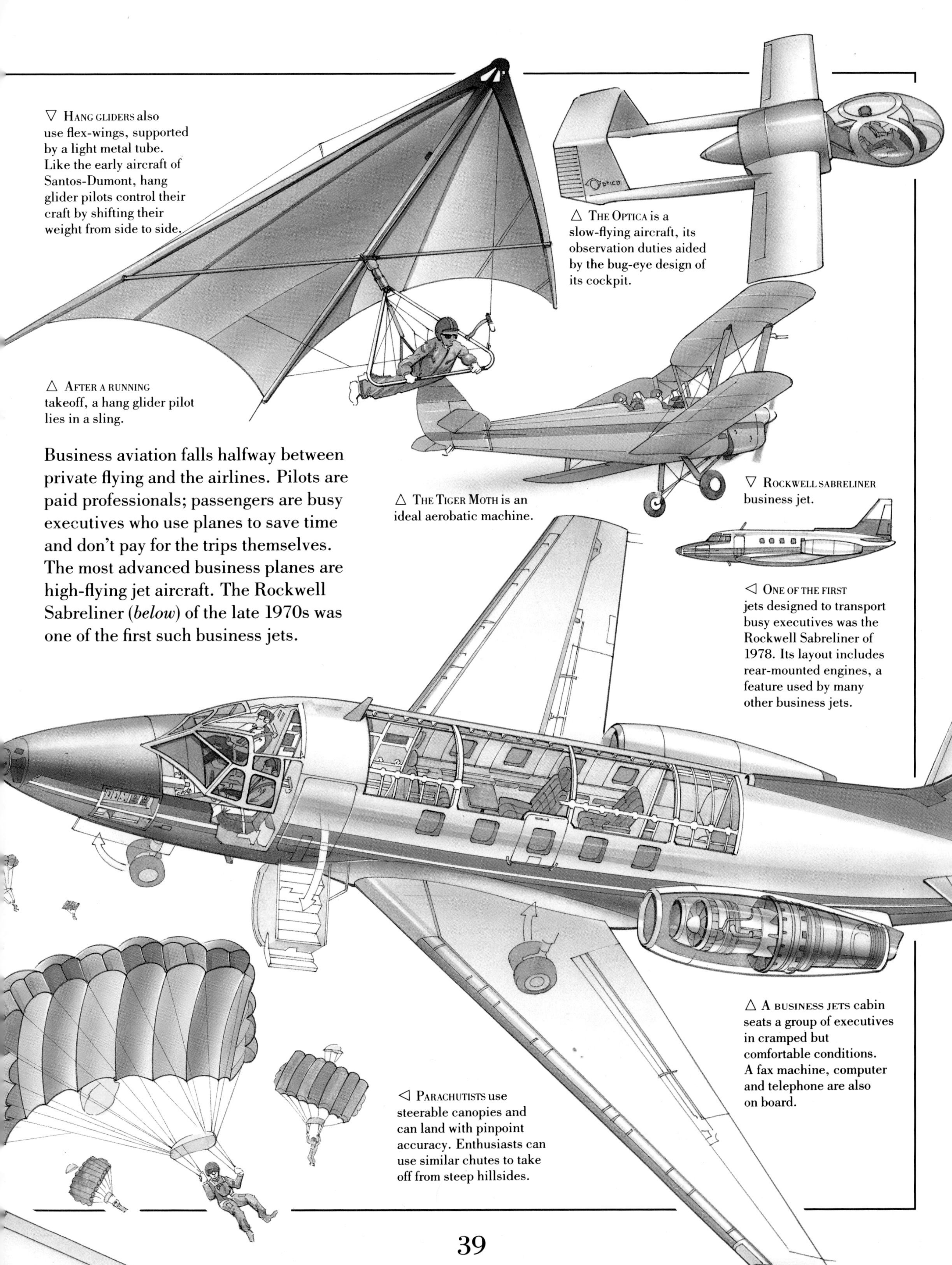

▽ HANG GLIDERS also use flex-wings, supported by a light metal tube. Like the early aircraft of Santos-Dumont, hang glider pilots control their craft by shifting their weight from side to side.

△ THE OPTICA is a slow-flying aircraft, its observation duties aided by the bug-eye design of its cockpit.

△ AFTER A RUNNING takeoff, a hang glider pilot lies in a sling.

Business aviation falls halfway between private flying and the airlines. Pilots are paid professionals; passengers are busy executives who use planes to save time and don't pay for the trips themselves. The most advanced business planes are high-flying jet aircraft. The Rockwell Sabreliner (*below*) of the late 1970s was one of the first such business jets.

△ THE TIGER MOTH is an ideal aerobatic machine.

▽ ROCKWELL SABRELINER business jet.

◁ ONE OF THE FIRST jets designed to transport busy executives was the Rockwell Sabreliner of 1978. Its layout includes rear-mounted engines, a feature used by many other business jets.

△ A BUSINESS JETS cabin seats a group of executives in cramped but comfortable conditions. A fax machine, computer and telephone are also on board.

◁ PARACHUTISTS use steerable canopies and can land with pinpoint accuracy. Enthusiasts can use similar chutes to take off from steep hillsides.

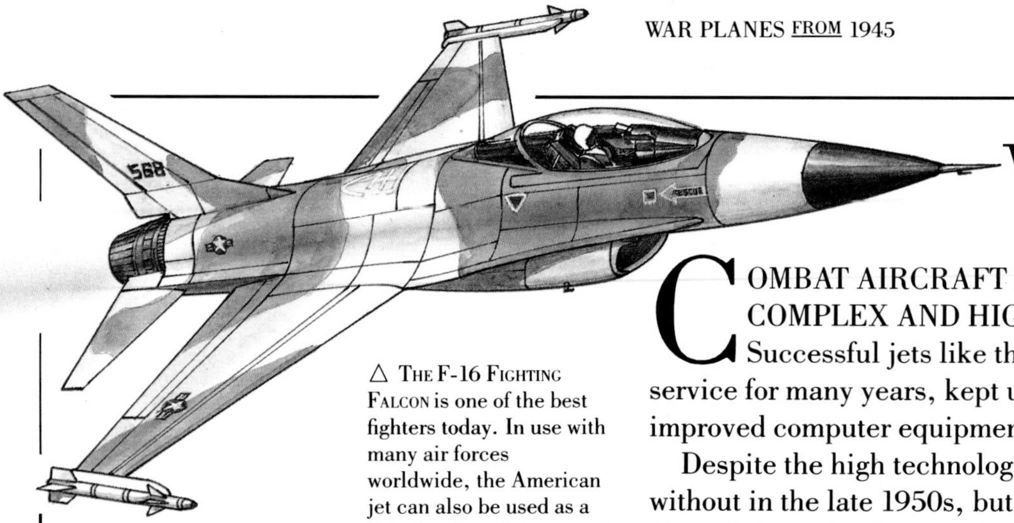

War Planes

COMBAT AIRCRAFT HAVE DEVELOPED INTO COMPLEX AND HIGHLY EXPENSIVE MACHINES. Successful jets like the Phantom II (*below*) can stay in service for many years, kept up to date by refitting them with improved computer equipment or new types of armament.

Despite the high technology, fighters still have guns. Some did without in the late 1950s, but experience in the Vietnam War showed that after the missiles were all fired, combat pilots still needed a gun in reserve. Other things remain the same, too: the best fighters are those that can outmaneuver their enemies.

△ THE F-16 FIGHTING FALCON is one of the best fighters today. In use with many air forces worldwide, the American jet can also be used as a light bomber. It is unusual for its air intake, which is mounted under the fuselage.

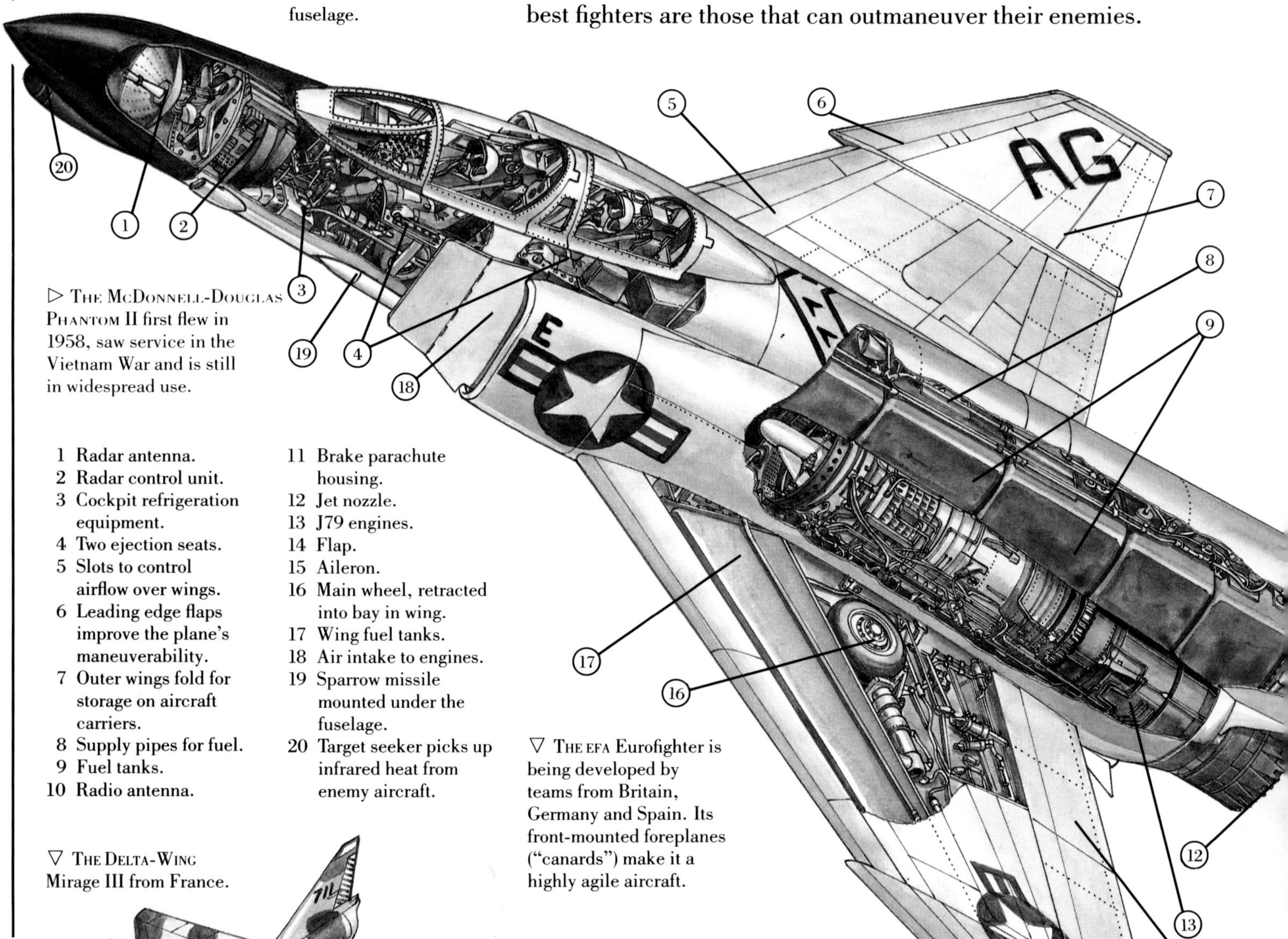

▷ THE MCDONNELL-DOUGLAS PHANTOM II first flew in 1958, saw service in the Vietnam War and is still in widespread use.

1 Radar antenna.
2 Radar control unit.
3 Cockpit refrigeration equipment.
4 Two ejection seats.
5 Slots to control airflow over wings.
6 Leading edge flaps improve the plane's maneuverability.
7 Outer wings fold for storage on aircraft carriers.
8 Supply pipes for fuel.
9 Fuel tanks.
10 Radio antenna.
11 Brake parachute housing.
12 Jet nozzle.
13 J79 engines.
14 Flap.
15 Aileron.
16 Main wheel, retracted into bay in wing.
17 Wing fuel tanks.
18 Air intake to engines.
19 Sparrow missile mounted under the fuselage.
20 Target seeker picks up infrared heat from enemy aircraft.

▽ THE DELTA-WING Mirage III from France.

▽ THE EFA Eurofighter is being developed by teams from Britain, Germany and Spain. Its front-mounted foreplanes ("canards") make it a highly agile aircraft.

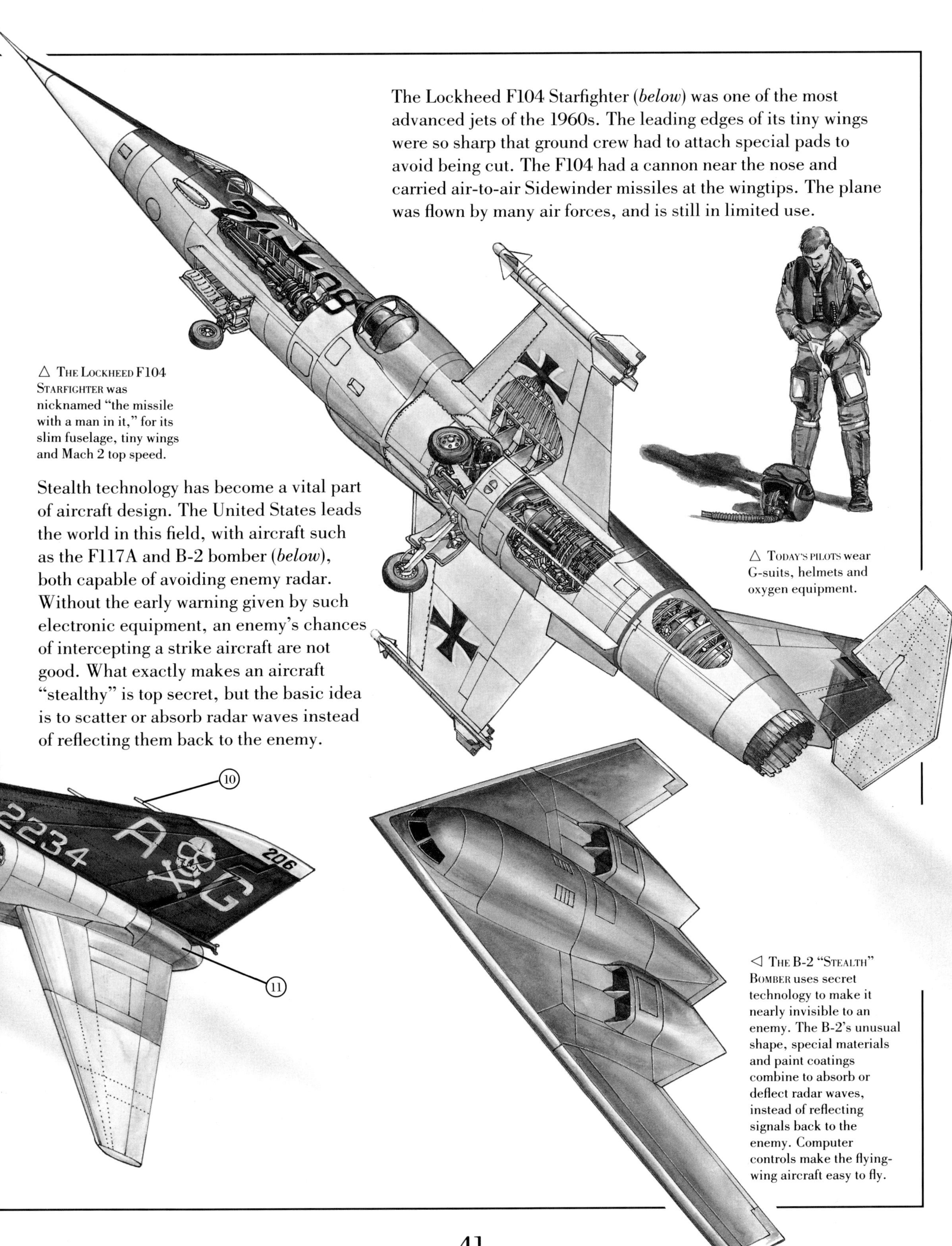

The Lockheed F104 Starfighter (*below*) was one of the most advanced jets of the 1960s. The leading edges of its tiny wings were so sharp that ground crew had to attach special pads to avoid being cut. The F104 had a cannon near the nose and carried air-to-air Sidewinder missiles at the wingtips. The plane was flown by many air forces, and is still in limited use.

△ The Lockheed F104 Starfighter was nicknamed "the missile with a man in it," for its slim fuselage, tiny wings and Mach 2 top speed.

△ Today's pilots wear G-suits, helmets and oxygen equipment.

Stealth technology has become a vital part of aircraft design. The United States leads the world in this field, with aircraft such as the F117A and B-2 bomber (*below*), both capable of avoiding enemy radar. Without the early warning given by such electronic equipment, an enemy's chances of intercepting a strike aircraft are not good. What exactly makes an aircraft "stealthy" is top secret, but the basic idea is to scatter or absorb radar waves instead of reflecting them back to the enemy.

◁ The B-2 "Stealth" Bomber uses secret technology to make it nearly invisible to an enemy. The B-2's unusual shape, special materials and paint coatings combine to absorb or deflect radar waves, instead of reflecting signals back to the enemy. Computer controls make the flying-wing aircraft easy to fly.

THE FUTURE

THE COMPUTER IS THE MACHINE THAT LINKS all the designs shown here. Future combat helicopters will use advanced computers for aiming and firing their weapons. Using such systems will require a sighting, using the helmet-aiming equipment. Then a spoken order to the airborne fire-control computer will launch missiles.

Highly agile aircraft like the YF-23 and X-29 are unstable in normal flight, and their moment-to-moment movements through the air can only be directed successfully by the lightning-fast reflexes of a computer-directed flight system.

The most powerful computers are used to help in the development of new aircraft. Designs can be "tested," by simulating their flight on video equipment, long before the real thing is rolled out from the construction works.

Computers are also used to cut the cost The idea is that by practicing on the ground in a very realistic "video game" simulator, a pilot can run through all sorts of flight exercises before trying them out for real, with no danger to life or aircraft.

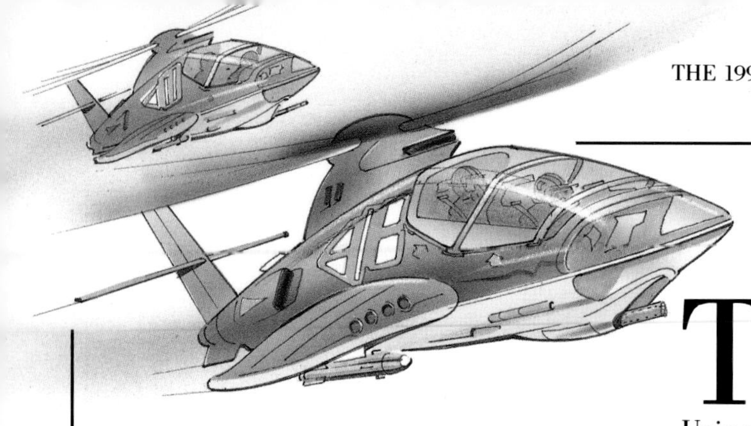

△ THESE STREAMLINED MACHINES are possible designs for future combat helicopters. High speed, computer controls and thick armor are features of this Bell/McDonnell Douglas design.

△ THE BOEING SIKORSKY LH is another design for a future combat helicopter. It resembles an updated version of the AH-64 Apache.

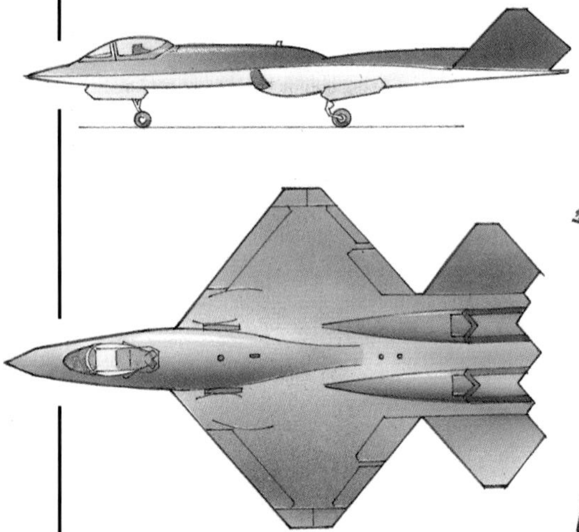

△ THE YF-23 (*top*) and YF-22 may be the look of fighters in the year 2000. Both craft can cruise at supersonic speed without needing an afterburner.

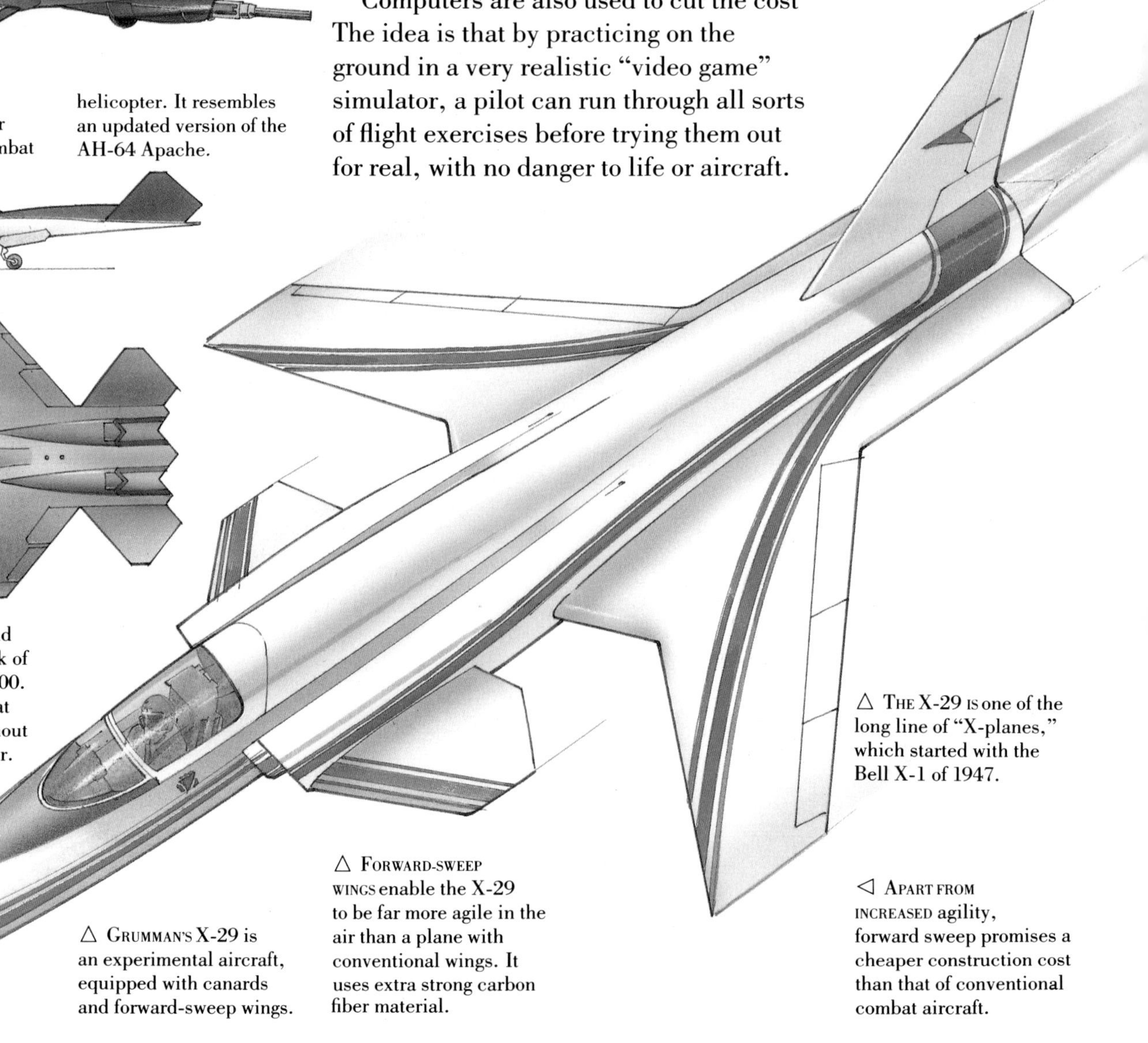

△ GRUMMAN'S X-29 is an experimental aircraft, equipped with canards and forward-sweep wings.

△ FORWARD-SWEEP WINGS enable the X-29 to be far more agile in the air than a plane with conventional wings. It uses extra strong carbon fiber material.

△ THE X-29 IS one of the long line of "X-planes," which started with the Bell X-1 of 1947.

◁ APART FROM INCREASED agility, forward sweep promises a cheaper construction cost than that of conventional combat aircraft.

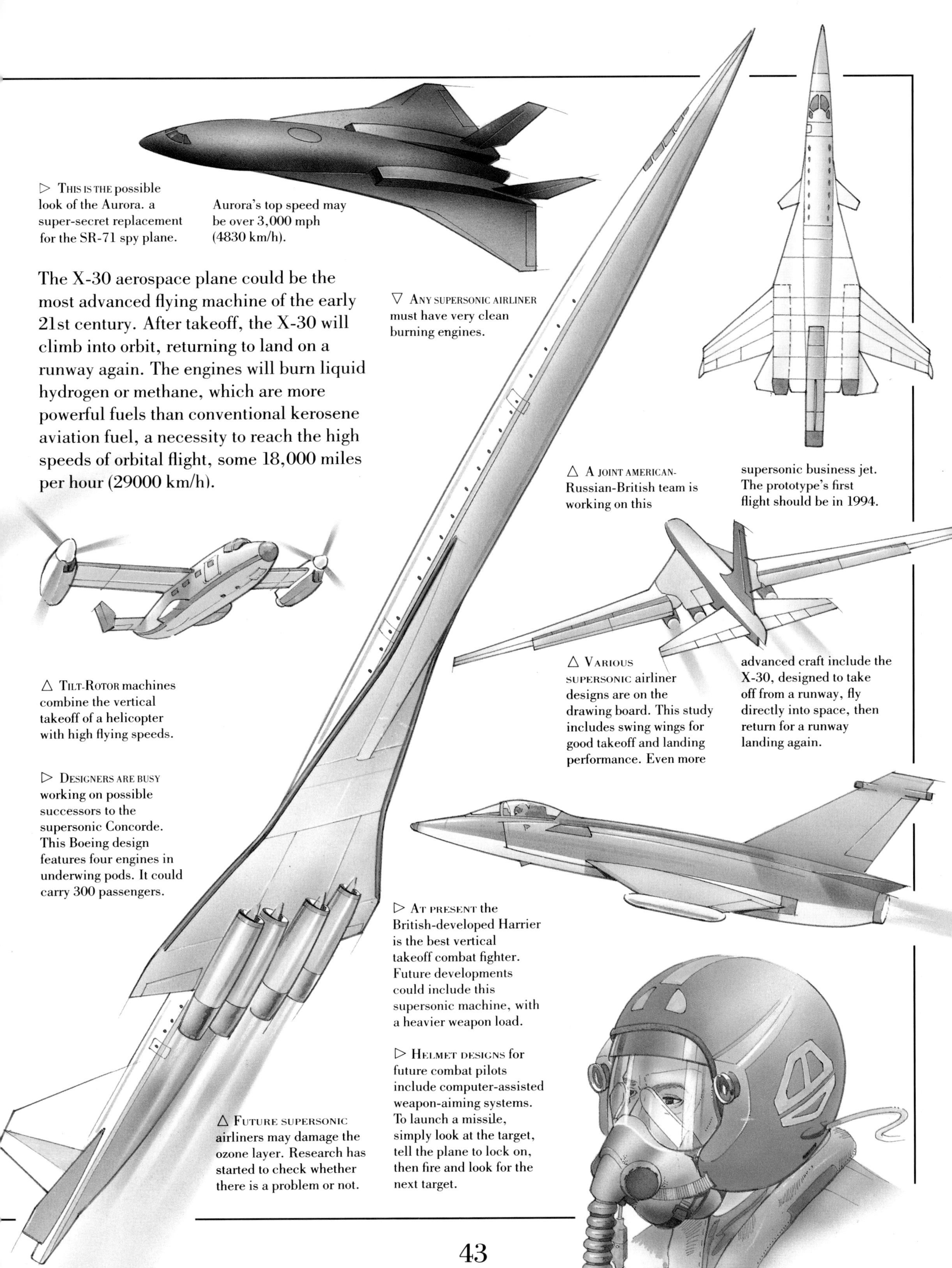

▷ THIS IS THE possible look of the Aurora. a super-secret replacement for the SR-71 spy plane.

Aurora's top speed may be over 3,000 mph (4830 km/h).

The X-30 aerospace plane could be the most advanced flying machine of the early 21st century. After takeoff, the X-30 will climb into orbit, returning to land on a runway again. The engines will burn liquid hydrogen or methane, which are more powerful fuels than conventional kerosene aviation fuel, a necessity to reach the high speeds of orbital flight, some 18,000 miles per hour (29000 km/h).

▽ ANY SUPERSONIC AIRLINER must have very clean burning engines.

△ A JOINT AMERICAN-Russian-British team is working on this supersonic business jet. The prototype's first flight should be in 1994.

△ TILT-ROTOR machines combine the vertical takeoff of a helicopter with high flying speeds.

△ VARIOUS SUPERSONIC airliner designs are on the drawing board. This study includes swing wings for good takeoff and landing performance. Even more advanced craft include the X-30, designed to take off from a runway, fly directly into space, then return for a runway landing again.

▷ DESIGNERS ARE BUSY working on possible successors to the supersonic Concorde. This Boeing design features four engines in underwing pods. It could carry 300 passengers.

▷ AT PRESENT the British-developed Harrier is the best vertical takeoff combat fighter. Future developments could include this supersonic machine, with a heavier weapon load.

▷ HELMET DESIGNS for future combat pilots include computer-assisted weapon-aiming systems. To launch a missile, simply look at the target, tell the plane to lock on, then fire and look for the next target.

△ FUTURE SUPERSONIC airliners may damage the ozone layer. Research has started to check whether there is a problem or not.

Timeline

Spirit of St. Louis, 1927

Icarus, Greek myth c 1000 B.C.

Tower jumper, Middle Ages

Montgolfier balloon, 1780s

Cayley glider, 1850s

Lilienthal commemoration disk, 19th century

BC
c.1000 The Greek myth of Icarus and his father Daedalus is written. In the story, Daedalus survives a flight over the Mediterranean Sea, while escaping imprisonment on the island of Crete. Icarus perishes: he flies too high and the sun's heat melts the wax which holds his wings together.
c.843 Bladud, King of Britain, killed while jumping from a tower, wearing a pair of feather wings.
c.400 Kites invented by the Chinese.
c.300 Carved wooden bird made, with an aerofoil section wing and tail fin. It was discovered in 1898 at Saqqara, Egypt, by a team of archaeologists.
AD
c.1020 The "flying monk," Oliver of Malmesbury, leaps from the top of an abbey wearing a pair of wings. He survives the glide, but a heavy landing breaks his legs. Various other "tower jumpers" try to fly, but all attempts end in failure.
c.1300 Merchant traveler Marco Polo sees demonstrations of man-carrying kites in China.
1783 Joseph and Etienne Montgolfier launch their first hot-air balloon. It leaves the ground on April 25 at Annonay in France, reaching a height of about 1,000 ft (305 m). The Montgolfier brothers' first public demonstration was also at Annonay. On June 4 of the same year, they release a small balloon from the market place. It reaches a height of 6,000 ft (1,830 m).
1850s Sir George

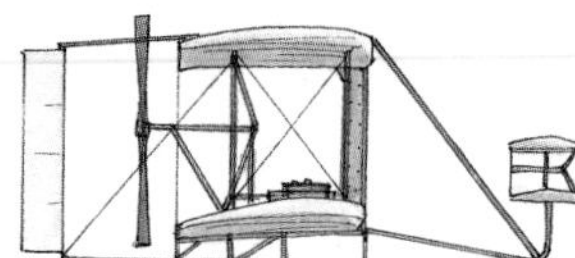

Wright Flyer, 1903

Cayley carries out gliding experiments at his home in Yorkshire. Cayley is now recognized as the father of modern aviation, as he set out many of the principles which govern heavier-than-air flight.
1890s German engineer Otto Lilienthal successfully tests a series of monoplanes and biplane gliders. A fatal

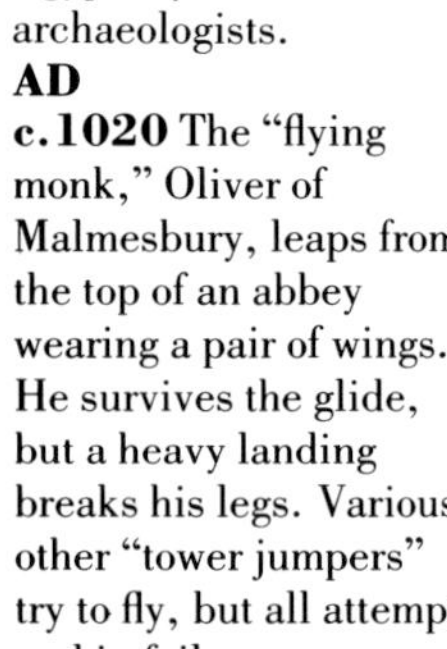
Fighter pilots, World War I

crash in 1896 ended his experiments before he could build a powered machine.
December 17, 1903 Wright *Flyer* becomes the first aircraft to achieve sustained flight with a man on board. The first hop covered a distance of 120 ft (36.5 m) and lasted about 12 seconds.
November 9, 1904 Wilbur Wright takes the *Flyer II* a distance of 2.75 miles (4.4 km). This was the first flight lasting over five minutes.

Martin flying boat, 1930s

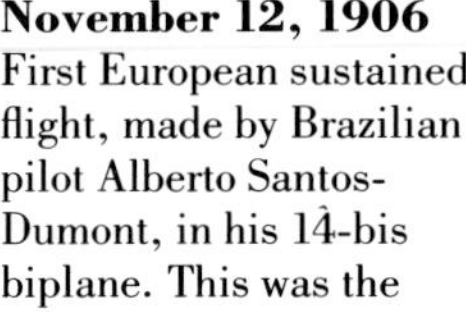

November 12, 1906 First European sustained flight, made by Brazilian pilot Alberto Santos-Dumont, in his 14-bis biplane. This was the first officially recognized

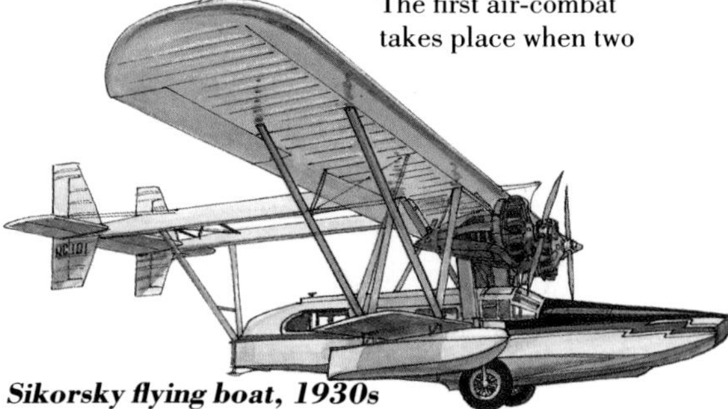
Sikorsky flying boat, 1930s

world distance record.
November 13, 1907 First free flight by a helicopter. Paul Cornu's machine hovered for 20 seconds near Lisieux in France.
May 14, 1908 Charles W. Furnas becomes the world's first air passenger, when taken for a half-minute flight by Wilbur Wright. The

P-51D Mustang fighter, World War II

first woman passenger was a Madame Peltier, who was taken aloft on July 8 in Italy. She was later the first woman to fly solo.
September 17, 1908 The first fatal air accident occurs when Orville Wright crashes in Virginia. He survives, but his passenger, Thomas Selfridge, is killed.
July 25, 1909 Louis Blériot successfully flies across the English Channel.
1912 The first single-seat scout aircraft, the Farnborough BS1, flies at 91 mph (147 km/h).

September 23, 1913 Roland Garros makes the first nonstop crossing of the Mediterranean Sea, a distance of 453 miles (730 km).
November 1913 The first air-combat takes place when two pilots exchange pistol shots during the Mexican civil war.
1914 First scheduled airline operation starts on New Year's day, from Tampa to St. Petersburg, Florida. The scheduled service lasts just four months.
August 30, 1914 First bombs to be dropped on a city. Five bombs from a German aircraft land on Paris.
October 5, 1914 Joseph Franz and Corporal Quenault, flying a Voisin, become the first aircrew to shoot down another aircraft, a

Bomber pilot, World War II

Bell X-1, 1947

German Aviatik. The greatest ace of the war was the Red Baron, Manfred von Richthofen, who shot down 80 aircraft. Rene Fonck was the Allies' best ace, with 75 confirmed victories.

February 5, 1919 Deutsche Luft-Reederei starts the first regular daily passenger service, between Berlin and

Cierva Autogiro, 1930s

Weimar in Germany.

May 1919 First transatlantic flight, by a US Navy NC-4, one of three to attempt the trip. The first nonstop flight was on June 14–15, 1919, by John Alcock and Arthur Whitten Brown, in a Vickers Vimy bomber fitted with long-range fuel tanks.

Eero Saarinen's TWA terminal at J.F.K. Airport.

October 7, 1919 KLM Royal Dutch Airlines founded. It is the oldest airline still flying under its original name.

April 7, 1922 Two airliners hit each other between London and Paris. This first mid-air collision forced authorities to devise the air lane system, in which airlines are allotted strictly regulated routes, times and schedules to avoid such tragedies.

1924 Two Douglas World Cruisers become the first aircraft to fly around the world. The trip (four planes started) took from April 6 to September 28.

May 20–21, 1927 Charles Lindbergh flies nonstop from New York to Paris, a distance of 3,610 miles (5,810 km). His speed averaged 107.5 mph (173 km/h).

May 1927 First flight of an autogiro, an aircraft using an unpowered rotor for lift.

July 25, 1929 Dornier Do X first flies. It was the largest flying boat built between the wars, with a passenger capacity of 150. The largest landplane at the time was the Junkers G38, with room for just 34 passengers.

November 28–29, 1929 First flight over the South Pole, by a Ford Trimotor. It was flown by Bernt Balchen, with Richard Byrd in charge.

May 15, 1930 Ellen Church becomes the first airline stewardess.

February 8, 1933 First flight of the Boeing 247, the ancestor of the modern airliner.

December 17, 1935 First flight of the Douglas DC-3, the most successful airliner ever.

June 26, 1936 Maiden flight of the Focke-Achgelis Fw 61, the first successful helicopter.

May 20, 1939 Pan American Airways' Boeing 314 Clipper starts the first regular airmail service across the North Atlantic.

August 27, 1939 Maiden flight of the Heinkel He 178, the world's first jet aircraft.

November 15, 1942 The German Heinkel He 219 night fighter is the world's first aircraft to be fitted with ejection seats as standard.

July 10, 1944 Messerschmitt Me 262 twin-jet fighter goes into service with the German Luftwaffe.

May 1945 Surrender of the most successful air ace ever, German pilot Erick Hartmann. His score was 352 enemy aircraft downed.

August 9, 1945 First atomic bomb dropped from a B-29 bomber on Hiroshima in Japan.

October 14, 1947 Bell X-1 *Glamorous Glennis*, piloted by Charles "Chuck" Yeager, breaks the sound barrier, at a speed of Mach 1.015.

July 27, 1949 Prototype of the de Havilland Comet 1 flies. This was the world's first jetliner, which entered service on May 2, 1952.

May 18, 1953 Jacqueline Cochrane becomes the first woman to go supersonic, flying a Sabre jet.

November 20, 1953 A Douglas Skyrocket research aircraft flies at twice the speed of sound, achieving Mach 2.005.

July 15, 1954 The Boeing Model 367-80 makes its first flight, later developed as a military tanker and as the 707 jetliner.

May 16, 1958 A Lockheed F-104A Starfighter establishes a new jet speed record of 1,403 mph (2,259 km/h).

October 21, 1960 First hovering flight of the British P1127 vertical takeoff jet. This aircraft was developed into the highly successful Harrier jet of today, still the only really successful vertical takeoff combat jet.

December 22, 1964 First flight of the Lockheed SR-71a Blackbird, the world's fastest military jet.

F-16 multi-role fighter

October 3, 1967 X-15A-2 rocket plane hits Mach 6.72, the fastest speed ever for a winged aircraft.

Sport parachute

March 2, 1969 First flight of the Aerospatiale Concorde supersonic airliner.

October 28, 1972 First flight of the Airbus A300 wide-body jetliner.

February 2, 1974 First flight of the General Dynamics YF-16. As the F16, the plane flies with the air forces of dozens of countries.

Concorde

August 23, 1977 First one-mile (1.6 km) figure-eight flight of a man-powered aircraft (MPA), the Gossamer Condor.

December 14, 1986 Rutan *Voyager* takes off on a round the world, unrefueled, flight. Dick Rutan and Jeana Yeager successfuly complete the trip nine days later.

January 1991 Lockheed F-117A is the first "stealth" aircraft used in combat during the Gulf War.

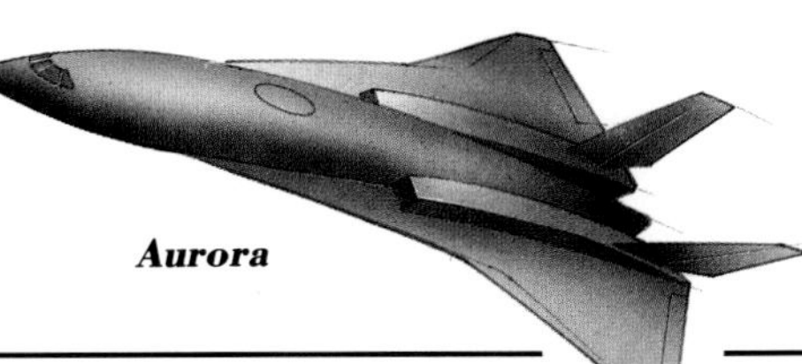

Aurora

Glossary

Aerofoil Any curving wing section that provides lift. In side view, an aerofoil has a curved upper surface, with a flatter lower side. Air flowing past is stretched out across the upper surface, which results in a partial vacuum or lower air pressure across the top. The wing is lifted into the air by a combination of vacuum suction on top and push from below.

Afterburner Part of a jet engine used to increase thrust for short periods, during take off and for combat emergencies. Fuel is sprayed into the jet exhaust, the "reheat" flame giving an instant power boost.

Ailerons Movable panels at the rear or trailing edge of an aircraft's wings. Moved up or down, they act as a pair to roll the plane to the left or right.

Air lane Route flown by airliners. Distances between aircraft are strictly controlled to avoid mid air collisions.

Autogiro A type of aircraft, halfway between a fixed-wing plane and a helicopter. An autogiro has rotor blades like a helicopter, but they are unpowered and spin like a windmill. Typically, an autogiro cannot land or take off vertically, but needs a short ground run before the rotor is spinning fast enough to give lift. Forward thrust is provided by a front-mounted engine and propeller.

Canard Front-mounted "tailplane" section, with elevators to control pitch. Used on the Wright *Flyer*, and occasional aircraft since.

Compressor blades Parts of a jet engine which compress or squash the air just before it is mixed with fuel and ignited in the combustion chamber.

Cowl helmet Type of helmet used in World War I to protect against frostbite on high altitude flights. Cowl helmets were aptly named, literally covering the head in an enveloping cowl of thick material. Goggles stopped the eyeballs from freezing solid.

Forward-sweep wing Swept wings are used for almost all high-speed aircraft because the shape delays the buildup of destructive shockwaves near the speed of sound. Forward-sweep wings reverse the direction of the familiar "swept back" wing to provide (in theory) a more maneuverable aircraft, important for a combat type. In fact, forward-sweep is experimental, and only possible using super-strong new materials such as carbon fiber resins.

Fuel injector In any engine, the part that sprays a mist of fuel into the combustion chamber. The resulting explosion moves a piston in a propeller engine, or provides a flaming exhaust in a jet engine.

Glider Aircraft with no engine, deriving its lift from rising air currents.

Interrupter gear World War I gear mechanism that timed forward-facing machine guns so that their bullets passed between spinning propeller blades instead of smashing into them.

Jet Type of engine that provides thrust by a powerful exhaust. Can be a turbojet or a turbofan, which has a large front fan which also gives thrust.

Load ring In a hot air or gas balloon, the metal ring that joins the basket to the lower half of the balloon.

Microlight A lightweight aircraft, typically less than 400 pounds without fuel, passenger or pilot.

Monoplane An aircraft with a single pair of wings. Other wing arrangements include biplanes, with two wings above each other, and triplanes, with three sets.

Pitch Nose up-and-down motion, provided in flight by moving the elevators on a tailplane or canard foreplanes.

Pod Smoothly-shaped section shaped to contain an aircraft part, typically an engine. Guns, electronic equipment and cameras can also be pod-mounted.

Prototype The first to be built of a new type of aircraft. Prototypes are test-flown to check flying characteristics. Any necessary changes can then be made before production aircraft start rolling off the assembly line.

Pusher prop A rear-mounted propeller, that pushes an aircraft along. Most aircraft with propellers have them mounted at the front, and are known as "tractor" props, because they pull the aircraft forward.

Retractable undercarriage Landing legs and wheels of an aircraft which are designed to fold away into the fuselage or wings in flight.

Ridge lift Air current blowing up the side of a hill. Gliders can use this type of rising air to keep aloft.

Roll Side-to-side rocking motion of an aircraft, controlled by the ailerons mounted on each wing.

Single shell fuselage Another word for monocoque construction, in which the skin of fuselage or body of the plane takes the stresses of flight. Early aircraft were constructed from wood strips, covered in fabric.

Squadron The basic fighting unit of an air force, consisting of a commander, pilots and their aircraft, together with the ground crews which are necessary to maintain the planes.

Supersonic Faster than the speed of sound. At sea level this is about 762 mph (1227 km/h), falling to 660 mph (1062 km/h) at high altitude.

Tailplane The fin, rudder and elevators of an aircraft. Also known as the empennage.

Thermal Rising bubble of warm air, used by glider pilots to gain height.

Triplane glider A type of three-winged glider designed by George Cayley for his flight experiments.

Turbine The spinning blades of a jet engine. Front turbines are used to suck in and compress air before ignition. A rear turbine spins in the exhaust to keep the front blades turning.

Vacuum sphere Concept devised by Francesco de Lana in the 17th century for lifting a flying machine above the ground. His idea was to make hollow spheres, which, because they contained no air, would be lighter than the surrounding atmosphere and thus float upwards. Sound theory, but in practice, the spheres would have been squashed flat by atmospheric pressure.

Yaw Swinging compass-movement of an aircraft away from the straight-ahead position. Controlled by the rudder.

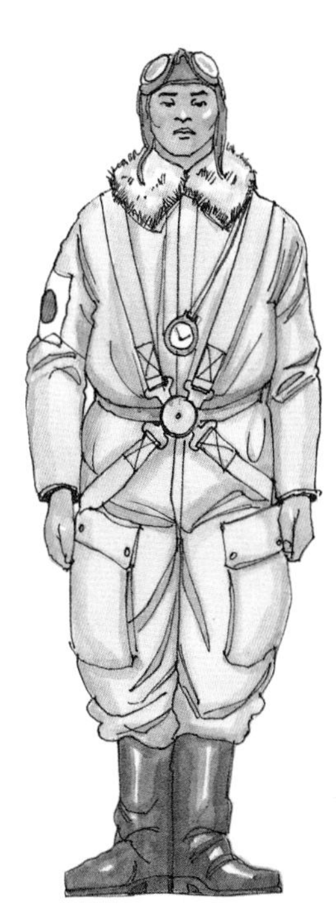

INDEX

Illustrations are shown by bold type. Names of airplanes are in italics.

PRINTED IN BELGIUM BY proost INTERNATIONAL BOOK PRODUCTION